Theodore Ledyard Cuyler

From the Nile to Norway and homeward

Theodore Ledyard Cuyler

From the Nile to Norway and homeward

ISBN/EAN: 9783337724283

Printed in Europe, USA, Canada, Australia, Japan

Cover: Foto ©ninafisch / pixelio.de

More available books at **www.hansebooks.com**

FROM

The Nile to Norway

AND HOMEWARD

BY

THEODORE L. CUYLER

PASTOR OF LAFAYETTE AVENUE CHURCH, BROOKLYN

NEW YORK:
HURST & COMPANY, Publishers,
122 Nassau Street.

Copyright, 1881,
By ROBERT CARTER & BROTHERS.

COPYRIGHT, 1891,
BY HURST & COMPANY.

ARGYLE PRESS,
Book Manufacturers,
265-267 Cherry St., N. Y.

TO

THE BELOVED FLOCK

WHOSE GENEROUS KINDNESS SENT ME ON THIS TOUR

THIS VOLUME IS

𝔊𝔯𝔞𝔱𝔢𝔣𝔲𝔩𝔩𝔶 𝔍𝔫𝔰𝔠𝔯𝔦𝔟𝔢𝔡.

CONTENTS

CHAP.		PAGE
I.	OUTWARD BOUND	9
II.	THROUGH ENGLAND AND FRANCE	19
III.	CRUISING IN THE MEDITERRANEAN	27
IV.	THE LAND OF THE PHARAOHS	43
V.	LIFE IN CAIRO	55
VI.	LAST VIEWS IN EGYPT	65
VII.	TO THE HOLY LAND	78
VIII.	WALKS ABOUT JERUSALEM	87
IX.	THE DEAD SEA AND THE JORDAN	97
X.	THE OLD AND THE NEW	108
XI.	BEYROUT AND THE SYRIAN MISSIONS	127
XII.	CHIO—AND A VISIT TO EPHESUS	139
XIII.	ON THE BOSPHORUS	149
XIV.	ATHENS	160
XV.	SUNRISE ON THE PARTHENON	171
XVI.	FROM ATHENS TO THE TYROL	181
XVII.	PRAGUE—DRESDEN	191
XVIII.	THE LAND OF LUTHER	201
XIX.	HAMBURG TO COPENHAGEN	210
XX.	THE CITY OF THORWALDSEN	219

CONTENTS.

CHAP.		PAGE.
XXI.	NORWAY.	227
XXII.	STOCKHOLM	239
XXIII.	THE WARM HEARTS OF SWEDEN	249
XXIV.	THE GREENTH OE ENGLAND.	262
XXV.	DRIVES ABOUT LONDON	271
XXVI.	CAMBRIDGE—THE SAVOY—MR. SPURGEON	281
XXVII.	DEAN STANLEY	292
XXVIII.	THE DRINK-QUESTION IN MANY LANDS	300
XXIX.	EXCURSIONS IN ENGLAND.	313
XXX.	A RUN INTO WALES	335
XXXI.	HOMEWARD	345

Biographical Sketch of the Author

By Professor EDWARD P. THWING, M. D., PH. D.

Some lives are monumental. They become historic before their earthly limit is reached. The author of this volume has a strongly marked personality. He puts it into all he writes. For this reason, largely, the productions of his pen, though fugitive and fragmentary, have entered into the religious literature of his time. The fecundity, freshness and versatility of his thought have given him a conspicuous place among the preachers and writers of the age.

THEODORE LEDYARD CUYLER was born at Aurora, N. Y., January 10, 1822, of Holland and Huguenot descent, and of a family of lawyers. His mother's prayer was that he might become a minister. Her first gift was a bible, which he was able to read at the age of four, when he became fatherless. At sixteen he entered Princeton and graduated in three years with honor; visited Europe, and was introduced to Dickens, Carlyle, Father Matthew and other prominent people. Graduating in 1846 from Princeton Seminary, he labored at Burlington and Trenton, seven years at Market Street, New York City, and for thirty years at Lafayette Avenue Presbyterian Church, Brooklyn. A jubilee volume published in 1885, and another on the occasion of his retirement from the pastorate, record the details of the ministry truly historic and rarely paralleled. The valedictory discourse given

April 6, 1890, is found in the Author's last volume, How to be a Pastor. It is a fitting close to the teachings of a timely treatise. Other books by Dr. Cuyler, are Stray Arrows, Cedar Christian, Empty Crib, Wayside Springs, Pointed Papers, Thought Hives, God's Light on Dark Clouds, Right to the Point, Heart Life and Newly Enlisted. Five of these are put into Swedish. His newspaper articles number thousands, and some of them have been reprinted in other languages, aggregating more than a hundred million copies. The titles indicate the picturesque form of his thought, even on the most serious themes. He has scarce a peer in this kind of rhetorical composition.

A frequent visitor in England and on the continent, on familiar terms with many social and religious celebrities, Dr Cuyler possesses opulent stores of information with which he enriches his articles descriptive of these travels. "FROM THE NILE TO NORWAY" illustrates the felicity of his diction and his keen powers of observation. These chapters were letters penned during his journey and sent home to a New York journal, week by week. The writer had the privilege of his company, during a portion of this tour, and was witness of the delight which his genial presence gave to the social circle, and the enthusiasm awakened by his public addresses.

The scope of the volume, the variety of topics treated, and the bright, breezy style of narrative will be appreciated by all who, in a book of travels, love to feel the constant touch of reality in every page. Though in his seventieth year, Dr. Cuyler's words lose none of their crispness and pungency, their beauty and vividness. Long may the dew of his youth continue, and his unresting pen give the world books as charming as this, "FROM THE NILE TO NORWAY."

BROOKLYN, 1891.

FROM THE NILE TO NORWAY.

I.

OUTWARD BOUND.

Near Queenstown, April 2, 1881.

IT was a raw March morning on which the stout ship "Bothnia" threw off her lines, and a cutting wind smote in the faces of the kind friends who gave us a parting cheer from the Cunard wharf. The vessel also was very cold for a few hours, but when the steam warmed up her iron ribs, she became thoroughly comfortable. As we steamed down the Bay, the other passengers were busy in getting off letters for the pilot; but my eyes were held fast to the spire of Lafayette-avenue Church, and when that beautiful and beloved landmark dropped out of sight behind Greenwood, I went below, and felt that the last link to home was broken off. The russet hills of Staten Island slowly disappeared; then the pasteboard palaces on Manhattan Beach; then we passed the light-ship, and were out on the great wide sea.

It has not grown any narrower since I first crossed it in the packet-ship "Patrick Henry" thirty-eight years ago, when I was a college-youth; but steam has put a carpeted cabin across the waves in half the time. In those days the "Independence" made a great run, under canvas, in fifteen days; but the average time was about twenty-five, except in winter; then old Boreas often boxed them about for forty days. The Bothnia is not famous for speed; but she is spacious, stout, and sociable. Captain McMickan's genial face throws a sunshine on her deck on the darkest morning, and Engineer Brown's violin can make the roughest night merry as a Christmas feast. We have four hundred and twenty feet for promenade, and a very genial company to keep step with in our daily walks. The steamer runs as true as a clock, and hardly varied from three hundred and twenty miles a day after we left Sandy Hook. At the Captain's table we have General Richmond, Consul at Rome, Colonel Richard Lathers, the Hon. Mr. Maxwell, and several other good sailors, who put in an appearance at every meal. My kind friend Mr. Howard Gibb, a Broadway merchant, presided at the opposite table; for he has crossed so often in the Bothnia that he has the freedom of the ship.

The most enjoyable time on board is the evening. Then a party of us assemble in Purser Wallace's room, and the Captain tells his full share of the lively stories which keep the room in a roar. Later in the evening we adjourn to the room of the chief engineer, Brown, who is a typical Scotchman, worthy of a place in one of Sir Walter's romances. Brown is not only a staunch Presbyterian, but a master of the violin; and the sight of him when he is pouring forth such old Scotch melodies as "Bonnie Doon," "John Anderson, my Jo," and "Come under my plaidie,' reminds one of the "Last Minstrel" when he played before the Duchess in old Branksome Tower. He puts his whole soul into the instrument whether the strains be grave or gay. So popular are his performances that his cabin is packed, and some of the ladies are glad to join our party and enjoy these delightful "nichts wi' Burns." More than one of my clerical brethren have lively memories of the Scotch stories and strains of Highland melody in the cosy room of Engineer Brown.

Last Sabbath was a day of storm. I fear that but few of our passengers greeted the morning with the familiar lines "Welcome sweet day of *rest*." The deck was spattered with the rain, and washed with the stray seas that combed over the bow. Only half the passengers were able to join with the Captain and crew at the morning service in the main saloon; even some of them beat a hasty retreat before the service was over. While the sailors were standing up to sing the psalm to old "Dundee," they swung to and fro like pendulums; and while I was preaching I had to hold on with both hands to the table. My theme was the "four anchors" which Paul's shipmates threw out during the tempestuous voyage to Rome. Nowhere do the good tidings of the Gospel sound more gladsome than on a dark and stormy day; and no souls have welcomed this Gospel more heartily than the men of the sea. It is a real luxury to preach to the blue-jackets in Mr. Williams' chapel at our navy yard; a sailors' prayer-meeting is a model for freedom and fervor. I trust that some fragments of divine truth may have been caught and retained by some of my auditors who held steadfastly to their seats in the uneasy cabin. One thing I feel sure of, and that is that no man ever preaches God's simple Word of life to even a handful of auditors without some results. No message faithfully spoken is left wholly unblest; no word returns to the divine Giver unless it have at least imposed a new responsibility on the souls that hear it. The old English liturgy is the common vehicle of devotion at all the services on these vessels; we all meet on the common ground of the Apostles' Creed, the Psalter, and Chrysostom's sweet, simple prayer; and as staunch a Presbyterian as my Scotch friend, Mr. Hugh Stirling, could join in the responses as heartily as my Episcopal neighbor, Colonel Lathers. On shore I prefer voluntary extemporaneous devotions; at sea I can appreciate Professor Hitchcock's arguments for a Book of Common Prayer.

Many of the passengers, in spite of the uneasy sea, occupy themselves with reading; but in addition to guide-books, the only volume that I have looked into is Froude's "Reminiscences of Carlyle." It is wonderfully characteristic; but the finest things in the book are his impassioned tributes to his "bonny little Jeannie," who shone around his grim head like an aureola, and whose bright look turned everything to gold. Just imagine the grizzly old bear of savage criticism (who did not spare even

Dr. Chalmers) breaking out into such lovely outbursts as this: "God reward thee, dear one! now when I cannot even own my debt. Thanks, darling, for your shining words and acts, which were continual in my eyes, and in no other mortal's. O! was it not beautiful, all this that I have lost forever?" Yes, it was beautiful; and ten thousand harsh and rasping utterances of Carlyle's pessimism can all be covered by the graceful mantle of his devoted, husbandly idolatry. Amid all the shams and "simulacra" of this degenerate world, the one bit of solid gold was the woman of his home and heart. We can forgive all the old growler's anathemas when we see him, at the age of fourscore, lying on the grave of his wife in Haddington kirk-yard, and kissing the turf that covered her.

I have been surprised that we have sighted so few vessels during this passage—not more than one or two each day. The reason probably is that the Cunard steamers have a track of their own, about fifty miles south of the great thoroughfare to Liverpool. The travelling public can well afford to take the longest route, when it affords them such an additional guarantee of safety. Well has this veteran line earned its crown of supremacy for perfect discipline, staunch steamers, and preservation of every single human life that has been committed to its charge for forty-one years!

I began this letter four days ago, when the winds were prosperous and the stout ship was pushing finely toward the "desired haven." But on Tuesday a savage head-wind took us by the throat, dashed the brine into our faces, and riled up the tempers of some of the passengers sadly. The rain and wind banished most of them from the deck and drove us down below to cultivate the grace of patience. I found it necessary to go around and visit my parishioners and cheer them up with all those consolations which have become stereotyped at sea in rough weather. Thanks to a free use, every morning, of Saratoga water, and to a careful diet, I have not been sea-sick. The traditional nonsense about warding off this dreaded malady by a liberal use of champagne or toddy, ought to be exploded. In this case, too, "wine is a mocker, and whoso is deceived thereby is not wise." A good aperient, light digestible food, and fresh air, are worth more than all the alcoholic potations ever concocted.

The horrible head-wind—which has thrown us thirty hours behind time—has not relaxed its grasp; but we are in sight of old Ireland —pride of all Irish patriots, prey of all Irish demagogues, and puzzle and plague of all English statesmen. The question now is whether she will allow Gladstone to help her out of her bottomless bog of difficulties. Patrick may well have a warm side for America; but for the relief that emigration to us has given to her surplus crowds, and for the myriads of "one-pound notes" sent hither by servants to the old folks at home, the Irish peasantry would have starved out long ago.

Grateful is the sight of her emerald shores. This chill, moist atmosphere brings no scent of April on its wings. England, Rome, the Alps, Athens and the Orient—all lie hidden beyond that wall of thin mist which overhangs the British Channel. May He who has brought us across the stormy sea, guide us through and beyond that veil, until our feet stand within thy gates, O Jerusalem!

II.

THROUGH ENGLAND AND FRANCE.

Marseilles, France, April 7, 1881.

IN all ages an east wind seems to have had a bad name. The Old Testament makes it a synonym for barrenness, and the New Testament a synonym for tempests; on the sea of Galilee it nearly wrecked the disciples, and on the Mediterranean, it hurled the Apostle Paul and his fellow-voyagers upon the beach among the broken fragments of their ship. The wind that took our steamer "Bothnia" by the teeth off the southern coast of Ireland, belonged to this unamiable family. It would not even allow us to halt, and leave our mails at Queenstown. So the Captain threw up signal-rockets, and we buffeted our way on towards Tuskar light in the face of the gale. By morning it had blown itself out of its passion; the sea grew quieter, so that the cabin was well filled at the Sabbath service; we entered the mouth of the Mersey at night-fall in a calm, and anchored there for the next rise of the tide. It was no pleasant thing at Liverpool to part from a genial company of passengers who could warm the wintriest day and cheer the darkest night in Lapland. Captain McMickan is a king on a quarter-deck.

We set off immediately for London by the North Western Railway which passes through some of the finest counties of England. The farmers were busy with plough and harrow; I fancied also that I saw shrewd "Mrs. Poyser" jogging along in her market-cart. It always thrills me,—when passing over this road—to look at the towers of Lichfield Cathedral in Dr. Johnson's early home, and at Lord Marmion's tower at Tamworth—and dear old Rugby School, famous for Dr. Arnold and Tom Brown—and at Berkhampstead, where Cowper first saw the light in the world he came to bless. We ran close to the hill of Harrow, from whose school went forth the wayward Byron, and the wise Sir Robert Peel. In five hours we were in roaring London. When I first saw London it contained two millions of people; now its uttermost limits contain four millions and a half. My beloved friend the Rev. Newman Hall was waiting to take me to his pleasant home on Hampstead Hill—a home once shadowed by peculiar trials, but now brightened with sweet domestic joys.

In the evening I went to the prayer-meeting of his congregation at Christ Church Westminster Road. Their edifice,—with its lofty Lincoln Tower, and its adjoining Hawkestone Hall—is more spacious and imposing than I had expected. The original founder of the church was Rowland Hill, and the remains of that eccentric but devoted minister of the Word have lately been removed from old Surrey Chapel, and deposited under the vestibule of the Lincoln Tower. A tablet in commemoration of our Martyr President is inserted in the wall; the Tower itself was erected by the joint contributions of the people of America and Britain. Mr. Hall took me up into the "Wilberforce Room" and the "Washington Room," which are used for Bible-classes. On the wall of the latter hangs a copy of our Declaration of Independence. Christ Church seats about two thousand, and it is usually full. The prayer-meetings are held in the portion of the building called Hawkestone Hall; on Monday evening last a large company were gathered, and we had an animated season of hand-shaking afterward, for that congregation and my own have long had an "evangelical alliance" on our own hook. Mr. Hall has a prodigious capacity for work, and on an average, delivers two or three discourses —over England—during every week, in addition to the charge of his large congregation, and its city-missions. After the delivery of His Sunday evening discourse, he goes out and preaches to an audience in the street.

As we drove back over Westminster bridge, the Thames embankment was ablaze with the new electric lights; and one also shone from the top of the tower of Westminster Palace to indicate that Parliament was in session. In fact while we were passing, Mr. Gladstone was just delivering his speech on the Budget to a crowd so dense that any attempt to get into the House of Commons were futile. The oratorical powers of the great Premier show no signs of decay; his campaign in Mid Lothian nearly two years ago may well be regarded as the grandest feat of political oratory in this century. During the time that the dexterous D'Israeli was astonishing the world with his juggleries, I often ventured the prediction, in public addresses, that Gladstone would again become the Premier of Great Britian. He owes his return to power very largely to the zealous support of the Presbyterians in Scotland, and the Nonconformists in England.

My stay in London was very brief, as I hope to revisit it in July. On Tuesday evening I took my share of the tossing in the termagant Channel on board of the boat for Calais. We reached Paris behind time and I hastened to the station for Marseilles. I had but a few moments at the station for conversation with Mr. and Mrs. Cogswell two faithful members of my church who are deeply interested in the evangelical movement now going on in Paris. Being desirous to see the most I could of them, I suggested that they should go through the ticket-door, and finish our talk in the car. The uniformed gateman stopped them, as they had no tickets. I promptly said to him, "Mes amis sont *Americains*. Vive la Republique." The man swung his hand enthusiastically and responded, "Vive la Republique!" and passed them through in an instant. I have found the word American to be an "open sesame" to more than one door in foreign lands. In every part of the world one can travel more pleasantly, and with more certainty of kindness from both the high and the humble if he lets it be known that he is a citizen of the United States. Occasionally I have met an American (of the shoddy species), who was very anxious to conceal his nationality—to the very great credit of his country.

My journey to Marseilles was by the lightning-express, which brought me five hundred and thirty-six miles in thirteen hours, running time! We ran through some of the most fertile and famous portions of La Belle France. From the car-window I saw ancient Dijon, the capital of Burgundy, the city of Charles the Bold and the birthplace of Bossuet. The door of the venerable cathedral was standing open, through which the great orator must have often passed in the days of his boyhood. We passed, quite too quickly, the historic reliques of Avignon, and the antique Arles with its Roman amphitheatre. The country was in all the glories of spring. At Dover, thirty-six hours ago, the trees were leafless. At Paris a faint touch of green began to appear. At Monteneau, the cherries and apricots were in full bloom. Above Lyons, the beautiful banks of the Saone were gorgeous with verdure and flowers. Here at Marseilles, everlasting spring abides, and the air is soft and balmy.

France is another land since that crowning mercy of Sedan. Never did a military defeat bring richer benefits to any land. The Ex-Empress cannot blind her eyes to the fact that France is vastly more happy, peaceful and prosperous under republican government than under the rule of her husband, the imperial charlatan. Protestantism is awakening to new life in many districts, and a new day is beginning to dawn upon the land of Coligny, and Lafayette and the Huguenots. The chief hindrance to the spread of Bible religion is the fact that so many of the thoughtful and cultivated classes associate the very name of Christianity, with the mummeries and priestcraft of ultramontane popery. Acute intellects in fleeing from superstition are carried over to infidelity; they make the transition too in almost utter ignorance of the solid middle ground of evangelical faith.

III.

CRUISING IN THE MEDITERRANEAN.

Bay of Naples, April 9.

IT was quite tantalizing to be hurried away so soon from beautiful Marseilles, which far surpassed my expectations. It is finely built, has 320,000 inhabitants, and a portion of it is Paris on a smaller scale. The Bourse would be a fine model for our public edifices. Of ancient cathedrals one sees a plenty in France; but the Cathedral of Marseilles is a new and magnificent structure in the Byzantine style. Perched on a lofty rock stands the "Notre Dame"—a church looking like a Gothic lighthouse; spiritually, the light is as darkness. The glory of the city is the park and its surrounding châteaux on the lofty heights which overlook the Mediterranean for many a league. The rich merchants enjoy up there what they earn in the town below.

We steamed out of the harbor of beautiful Marseilles at twelve o'clock on Thursday. As everybody is coming away from the Orient at this season of the year, and nobody is going, the eastward-bound boats run empty. In the spacious first-class saloon of this large steamer I am to-day monarch of all I survey. I have thirty or forty staterooms at my command. The polite steward, who jabbers French at me, devotes his exclusive labors to keeping my solitary room in order. He rings the bell for breakfast long and loud at 9 A. M., and for dinner at 5 P. M.; and all this superfluous racket is made in order to summon one diminutive parson to the table. When there, I am supported on the right, by the captain—who wears three stars on his coat-collar—and on the left hand by the purser in his jaunty blue uniform, but no stars at all. They rattle away in French, and leave me to my meals and my meditations. The captain occasionally shies a bit of broken English at my head, and I fire back a small volley of equally broken French.

While I am quite alone in the first cabin, there are seven passengers in the second cabin—whose accommodations are just as good but not quite as showy as in the first. One of these is a very genial Welshman, Mr. Humphrey Jones, who is going on commercial business to Alexandria. There are two French Jesuit priests on board, who "having no place" in France, are bound for Cairo and Abyssinia on a mission to the natives. They are bright cheerful fellows (whose adopted names since they were admitted to the "Society of Jesus," I have not learned), and they are very constant in the study of their guide-books. The younger one is handsome, affable, and looks as if he could not twist a thumb-screw, if he had one. They are picking up English, and are very much inclined to be sociable. I could not but pity the poor wifeless homeless creatures as they go roaming around the world on their embassies of craft, at the bidding of their ecclesiastical superior.

For two days we have enjoyed the poetry

of voyaging over a sea as smooth as New York harbor, and in view of shores that were famous in the days of Cæsar and Virgil. Yesterday morning I looked out of my window—or "port" more properly—and saw the villages and mountains of the island of Corsica. Snow-clad peaks crowned the centre of the island. On the southern end, in the town of Ajaccio, a man-child was born (in August, 1769), who was destined to turn this world upside down in his mad ambitions. This whole region was vivid with memories of Napoleon. The afternoon previous we had sailed past Toulon, where in his youth he had learned how to blow his fellow-men into eternity from the mouth of a cannon. The artillery practice he learned at Toulon, he perfected at Austerlitz and Jena. Soon after leaving Corsica, we ran close in by a wild volcanic island on whose mountain-sides were a few scattered vineyards. That bleak and desolate spot was the famous Elba, to which the man of blood was banished in 1814. What fools the Allies were to suppose that they could keep the Minotaur chained up on the island which was almost in sight of France. The bleak cliffs of Elba wore an aspect to me of sullen gloom, as if the portentous shadows of Waterloo were still brooding over them.

What a blessed thing for France it is that the last bubble of Bonapartism has exploded, and the race has run out forever! One thing is pretty certain, there can be no more revival of the Napoleon dynasty, and no more tricks played under the disguise of the famous cocked hat and gray riding-coat. France has got a taste of the cup of constitutional liberty, and she is not likely to return to a wallowing in the mire of Imperialism. Great advance is being made in popular education. Railways are bringing new ideas into the rustic secluded regions. The press is free. Best of all, the buried roots of Protestant Christianity are beginning to sprout up again into a new life—to be nourished and watered by the zeal and the prayers of such men as McAll and Fisch and Réveillaud. Our brother, Dr. Hitchcock, is doing his full share in this noble work—and has well earned the holiday vacation he is about to take in America. Give him the welcome he deserves.

All day we ran from Corsica southward through a succession of picturesque islands. Nearly every one bore marks of volcanic origin. Some contained nothing visible but a single lighthouse. Others were sprinkled with a few houses and vineyards. One of them showed a town with church-towers, and sails in its tiny harbor. They lie along the great pathways of war and commerce since the days of Hannibal, and the times when the Roman galleys went off through these seas to the conquest of the East. Yet they are almost unknown to the busy world of these days, which still sails past them and leaves their fishermen and vine-dressers to their primitive seclusions.

Thus far I am very much pleased with this route to Egypt. The steamer "Moeris" is one of the fleet belonging to the "Messageries Maritimes," a French company who are the Cunards of the Mediterranean. Their boats are excellent in all their appointments, well manned, with large state-rooms and every luxury with which the leviathan of sea-life is tamed and domesticated. They leave Marseilles on every Thursday, and reach Alexandria in six days. This is a preferable route, on some accounts, to the one by Brindisi. It affords a view of some of the finest scenery of the Mediterranean, and avoids the stupid journey down the east side of Italy. A halt is also made for six hours in the peerless Bay of Naples. From that point we head southward to the Straits of Messina, run in sight of Stromboli and Mount Ætna, and take the track of the great Apostle on his way to Rome. Yesterday we were on the pathway of Napoleon; to-day we are on the track of Paul. God never created two more richly endowed men than they; but in the last great day of reckoning, oh what a difference!

We are approaching Naples. Old Vesuvius keeps his signal-fires blazing—except while his wrath smoulders within his ribs, and sends out a sullen smoke. His crest looked down on Paul the prisoner when he landed at yonder Puteoli and was led away towards Rome. Through what changes have I passed in a single week! Six days ago on the cold, stormy Atlantic; since then, Liverpool, the hedgerows of England, London, Paris, the orchards and vineyards of sunny France, the distant glimpses of the Alps, the islands of the Mediterranean, and now in the morning light Naples opens her Gate Beautiful to give us welcome! Like the old voyager of eighteen centuries ago when he landed here, let us "thank God and take courage."

April 13.

The tourist who wishes to preserve the æsthetic illusion which overhangs Naples had better remain on board, and not venture on shore; the man must have studied the city from the water who first said, "See Naples, and then die." Having never seen it, I decided to make the venture, especially as so many urgent invitations were shouted at me from every side.

As soon as we had tied up to the buoy in the magnificent harbor, we were surrounded by a swarm of clumsy little boats, filled with that indescribable class of humanity called the "lazzaroni." "Dese are vot you call de *vagabonds*," said the Neapolitan guide to me as we pulled off for the shore. In the same boat with us were the two Jesuits, and a flap-hatted nun, who left us at Naples. The Jesuits went on shore to pay their respects to the Archbishop and to attend the service of mass.

As soon as we landed I pushed in among the narrow, crowded, filthy streets, not over a dozen feet wide, and blocked up with swarms of men, women, children, and donkeys. Not one of the rabble looked as if he, she, or it had ever seen a square inch of soap. They were a vagrant mass of unmitigated nastiness. How the creatures live is a mystery; but cheap fruits and maccaroni constitute their chief subsistence at a cost of a sixpence a day. Emerging from these narrow gangways I reached the Corso Toledo, which is the principal street of Naples. Thence I went on to the Santo Carlo Opera House and the Royal Palace. This latter superfluity is only used now when Humbert, the king of united Italy, pays a visit to his southern territory. It used to be the residence of the villainous King Bomba; and up on the hill above stands the ancient Castle of San Remo, which he used as a Bastile, and which Garibaldi broke open to the daylight. Beyond the Palace I came down to the handsome street which faces on the bay, and is lined with the principal hotels. This part of the city is modern, and comparatively clean.

Naples does not compare with Marseilles for architectural beauty. None of its two hundred and sixty churches is remarkable for anything but gilded and frescoed ceilings, pictures by the square rod, and crowds of ill-clad worshippers. It is the paradise of Popery, with swarms of idle priests, who lord it over an idle populace. When the millennium comes, Naples will be one of the last to yield to the gospel.

But from the steamer's deck the city was brilliant with color and picturesque forms. It stretched before us like a crescent, with its hills crowned with villas and pines; at either extreme were Posillippo with its cavern, and Sorrento with its vineyards and olives. I sat on the deck for three hours, and feasted on the magnificent panorama. The beauty of the whole was wonderful— the dirt of the details was invisible from that distance. Vesuvius curled up his languid smoke gracefully to the clouds. Pompeii—which must have been a cultured Sodom in its obscenity and idolatries—lies at its southern base. Capri lifted its rocky crest out of the smooth sea.

We enjoyed this peerless panorama until two o'clock, and then the last of the lazzaroni pulled off in his clumsy boat, we hoisted anchor, and steamed down the

Bay. In an hour we were abreast of the island of Capri, where the Emperor Tiberius had his palace and his revelries. Away off to the northeast we could dimly discern Puteoli, the spot on which Paul set foot when he was greeted by the brethren, who besought him to tarry with them seven days. We were now fairly upon the great Apostle's track.

During the evening we passed Stromboli, the dull red glare of whose volcano is visible for many leagues. Vesuvius commonly emits but a faint flame; Stromboli seems to have a larger supply of fuel. On Sabbath morning we were running close to the coast of Calabria, and the "Rhegium," toward which Paul's captain "fetched his compass," was on our left. The coast is rocky, but here and there small towns nestle among the cliffs and the stretch of faint green slopes. Then we passed between Scylla and Charybdis, and the shores of Sicily appeared on our right. It was too misty to catch a glimpse of Mount Ætna, although its crest rises above ten thousand feet. A little to the south of it lies old historic Syracuse, where Archimedes first cried "Eureka!" where Athens fought her great naval fight, and where Paul landed and tarried for three days. It was a source of real regret to me that the steamers of this line do not take Malta in their way. We were intensely anxious to see the island on which Paul and his shipwrecked fellow-voyagers escaped safe to land, some on boards and some on broken pieces of the ship. The spot is now known as "St. Paul's Harbor" and the soundings at the present day correspond exactly to those which are described in the twenty-seventh chapter of the Acts. The monks of Malta pretend to show the cavern in which the Apostle found refuge. It is rather remarkable that they should not exhibit the original viper that fastened on his hand, well-preserved in a bottle of spirits.

But, if we did not see the site of Paul's shipwreck, we had a small taste of his experience. All the way from Puteoli we had a gentle southerly breeze and tranquil seas, but soon after we entered the mouth of the Adriatic (or that part of the Mediterranean which was anciently called "Adria") a fierce east wind began to blow. If it was not as violent as the "Euroclydon," it came from the same quarter. All day on Monday we were tossed "up and down in Adria." The seas ran so high that my half-dozen fellow-passengers were glad to betake themselves to their berths, and I experienced the only taste of genuine sea-sickness that I have suffered from since I left New York. The two Jesuit priests—who are on their way to Egypt to conduct some ecclesiastical diplomacy on the Upper Nile—did not make their appearance on deck during the whole day. With some faint show of courage, I came to the dinner-table, with the captain and purser; but, after a few spoonfuls of soup, I was glad to retire to private life Unless Paul had a miraculous preservation from sea-sickness, I will warrant that his heroic stomach had some terrible qualms when he was weathering through that fourteen days of tempest. His water-soaked biscuit must have gone down rather toughly, when I found it so difficult to manage dainty soups, and broiled chickens, and oranges.

Towards evening on Monday the east winds abated. We were "sailing close by Crete," over the very waters which the great Apostle traversed before the Euroclydon burst forth in its fury. Although so close to the shore, we could only catch a faint view of the mountains of the island. "Salmone" is still the name of the cape at the eastern end. Soon after midnight we sighted the lighthouse on the southern shore of the island, and as its twinkling lantern sunk down behind the waves we lost sight of the last spot that is identified with the old hero on our present route. We leave Cyprus far to the north; and, although ours is a "ship of Alexandria," its sign is not "Castor and Pollux," and it carries one Presbyterian parson and two popish priests, instead of an apostle to the Gentiles.

Yesterday the sun came out brightly. We have been running over seas that danced and sparkled in his rays. From the deck we can look out over the waters which were once traversed by the ships of Tyre, by the galleys of proud Rome, and by the fleets that brought the wealth of the Orient to Venice. All these are forgotten; but the world will always hallow the memory of that one old corn-ship, which was tossed about in these waves for many dark nights, and yet could not sink while it upheld the life of the glorious man who was yet to "stand before Cæsar."

IV.

THE LAND OF THE PHARAOHS.

Cairo, April 15.

ON Wednesday morning—our sixth from Marseilles—we came in sight of Pompey's Pillar and the tall lighthouse, which mark the site of Alexandria; but it lies so low on the sands that it seems to sleep on the surface of the sea. It gives one a keen thrill to see the famous old city which was the scene of the exploits of Alexander the Great and Julius Cæsar in ancient times, and of Napoleon and Lord Nelson in modern times—the city in which the Septuagint was completed, and Origen and Cyril and Athanasius delved in theological lore. The Alexandria of to-day is a busy, bustling combination of all ages, customs, tongues and nationalities. In the same street you may see a Mohammedan mosque, a tasteful,

Parisian-looking mansion, and an "American Bar-room" for the sale of juleps and sherry-cobblers! The entrance to the harbor is picturesque. Napoleon's windmills on the sandy shore—still whirling briskly—and the tall pillar built by Pompey, the Roman prefect, are among the most conspicuous objects. We swung round the end of the breakwater, and shot in among some Egyptian war-vessels and the Khedive's large and superb steam-yacht, which is said to run over twenty miles an hour.

Swarms of Arab boats put off to meet us—a half dozen boats to each passenger. I soon detected a crew of fellows on whose white tunics was embroidered "Cook's Boatmen." I hailed them at once; Calipha Hassein, their polite Arab captain, in blue gown and red tarboosh, took me in charge and pulled me away rapidly to the Custom House wharf. I was put through the passport and customs offices in a twinkling, and in twenty minutes from the time that I left the deck of the "Moeris" I was snugly fixed in the

Hotel d'Europe on the Great Square of Mehemet Ali. Here let me say that I am traveling through the East with Cook's tickets, and I find three good arguments for using them. They are economical, they insure prompt attention everywhere, and they save you often the vexation of buying tickets from railway and other officials who speak in unknown tongues. The senior Thomas Cook is an old friend and fellow-worker in the Temperance movement for twenty years.

But what a sensation is the first half hour which an American spends in an Oriental city! The "Arabian Nights" of our boyhood are all reproduced before us. Here are the water-carriers and the cross-legged tailors, and the old turbaned Turk selling his shibooks; here is Fatima peering with her black eyes over the outlandish veil that hides her brown visage; and here is Aladdin himself, in blue gown and a jaunty, red sash twisted around his saucy head. Hundreds of costumes appear—no two exactly alike

—from an European suit, crowned by a red-tasseled fez cap, to a white-shirted Nubian, and so on to the identical garb that Abraham may have worn on the plains of Mamre. The streets, the markets, the bazaars are a perfect kaleidoscope of novelties and fun. Bunyan's "Mr. Despondency" could not have refrained from a laugh if he had seen that huge Arab in white robe and green turban, and with his bare, brown legs, as he trots briskly by on a donkey not three feet high. I did nothing but laugh while in the streets of Alexandria, and I do not expect to stop till I leave Cairo. It is enough to cure a chronic dyspeptic.

I took the train for Cairo at two o'clock, and found it a very fair reproduction of English management in a land where a locomotive seems as much out of its latitude as a camel in Broadway. I observed that the engine bore the mark "Stephenson & Co., Newcastle-on-Tyne." That was the early home of the celebrated Stephenson, the father of modern railways. The train was largely occupied by Egyptians, and the third-class cars were a perfect menagerie of Nubians, Arabs, and every variety of people in every variety of outré costume. They were a merry crowd, laughing, gabbling and smoking. The road runs through the Delta which is the garden of Egypt—producing at this season vast crops of barley, wheat, millet and various vegetables of whose name and nature I have no idea. Palm-trees skirt the way, with long lines of tamarisk. Occasionally the minaret of a mosque came in sight across the broad fields—which are even more level than Long Island is about Rockaway and Jamaica.

All the way to Cairo presented a series of charming pictures that to my unpractised eye was a perpetual delight. Here was a group of peasant women filling their water-jars from one of the innumerable small canals; some walked off like Rebekahs in flowing robes with the jars upon their heads. Here was a buffalo slowly turning the water-wheels that irrigate the level fields. Then came a procession of ambling camels, laden with enormous loads of green fodder: a grinning Arab boy perched on the load. Then trotted past a turbaned Copt, or a half dozen Arabs on their diminutive donkeys, each rider sitting as near the animal's tail as possible without being "left astern." Some respectable towns were passed, like Tantah and Birket es-Sab, each of which displays a flashy palace of the Khedive. But the most remarkable objects are the Arab villages—mere agglomerations of mud-hovels, packed closely together, with apertures for the Fellaheen and their brown children to creep in. At a distance they looked like a lot of magnified prairie-dogs dodging into their holes. Around each of these rude villages were a few date-palms, and often a small minaret rose above the heaps of mud. Yet these peasants were a happy, and often a fine, bright-looking class; all seemed to be busy with their primitive husbandries of ploughing, irrigating, driving their camels, or tending their small flocks of sheep and goats. We crossed both branches of the Nile, on fine iron bridges, and I felt like doffing my hat in reverence to this most venerable of all the rivers on the globe. If it was as muddy in the times of Moses, he must have needed a well-caulked ark of bulrushes.

A magnificent moonlight flooded the domes and minarets of Cairo as we approached this wonderful city. At the station the large carryall of Shepheard's Hotel met the train, and we were driven through streets brilliantly lighted and among crowds of noisy donkey-drivers to the west side of Esbekeeyeh Park. This hotel—the rendezvous of English-speaking tourists—is an Oriental-looking establishment, with an interior garden filled with palms, figs, and pomegranates. One of the polite landlord's first salutations was, "Ah, sir, I have seen your name in the *New York Herald* in a letter to Mons. Crosby." How far those twain candles have thrown their beams!

Yesterday was comfortable, although a week ago the "khamseen," or sorocco, scorched Cairo with a temperature of ninety-five. I expect some hot work before I get out of the Levant. My first step here was to look up my old friend General Batcheller, who is a member of the staff of Judges who preside in the court in yonder Palace of Justice. General Batcheller is the American member of that tribunal. I was piloted to his residence, in the elegant modern quarter, by Ali Hassan, my donkey-sergeant, and one of the most voluble of the sons of Ishmael. He pointed with pride to a squad of donkeys, and said, "Yonder black donkey is de one you shall ride, sar; he be berry easy, and his name be Yankee Doodle Dandy." I suspect that the little brute changes his name to suit the nationality of his rider. Outside of Ireland there is nothing that can surpass the vivacious blarney of a Cairo dragoman or donkey-boy.

In the afternoon General Batcheller drove me to the lofty citadel of Cairo (built by

Saladin in 1160), which commands the finest view of the city and the Pyramids. Close by it is the superb mosque of Mohammed Ali—whose pillars are of solid alabaster, and whose walls are faced with the same material. Some criticise this structure as too gorgeous, but as the light poured into the gilded dome through the stained glass, it seemed to my eye a perfect dream of Oriental poetry wrought in gold and alabaster. On our way through the crowded "Mooskee" we met a wedding procession, headed by a band of music, and followed by a troop of Arab boys. The bride was literally *encased* in a flashy suit of vermilion and silver —not an eyelash visible! She was led by the hand under a crimson canopy, and an hour after we met the procession again, still "toiling on" through the crowded streets. Last evening the bridegroom set out on his march, with lamps and torches, to wed the young wife whom his eyes had never beheld! He had won her by bargains, and not by courtship. That picturesque procession going forth to meet the bridegroom was but another photographic scene from Scripture, such as pass before one every day in these ancient birth-lands of the Bible. After nightfall I set out on a stroll through Cairo and was struck with the quietness and good order of every part of the city which I traversed. It is said that a stranger can go anywhere at night without any danger of molestation; if he loses his way he has but to call one of the ubiquitous donkey-boys who will soon trot him back to his hotel. I saw no dram-shops filled with carousers, and encountered no abandoned characters making night hideous with their harlotries. If Cairo is infected with the "social vice," it hides the leprosy from public view. Mohammedanism degrades woman in many ways, but it does not put her to the open shame which so shocks us in the thoroughfares of London or Liverpool or of too many towns in America.

In front of the brightly lighted cafès I saw groups of smokers enjoying their cigarettes, or languidly puffing their narguilèhs. In some of the smaller cafès a story-teller was entertaining a group of listeners. The Arab is as fond of listening to marvellous tales as he was in the times when the "Arabian Nights' Entertainments" were composed. Even those stories themselves about "Sinbad" and about the "Forty Thieves" are still eagerly welcomed. They will devour anything and everything that takes the form of a story. Sometimes one of our missionaries drops in at a cafè, and tells the story of Joseph, or one of the parables of the New Testament, and always finds a most respectful and attentive audience. This fact throws its side-light upon the genuineness of Scripture; for as the Oriental tastes of to-day are the same as in ancient times, it explains to us the frequency with which narratives and parables were used by the prophets and by the Divine Teacher himself.

These first two days in Egypt have brought with them an excitement that scarcely allows me to quiet down to sleep. It seems like an exhilarating dream that I am actually in the land of Moses, and the Pharaohs—that the turbid stream which I saw from the citadel to-day was grandfather Nile—and that these streets have echoed to the hoofs of Saladin's cavalry. We must make the most of such antiquities as Egypt now contains; for the Arabic art of to-day seems as incapable to reproduce such a structure as the Mosque of Sultan Hassein as it is to build another temple of Luxor, or to pile another Pyramid.

V.

LIFE IN CAIRO.

Shepheard's Hotel, Cairo, April 18.

A FRIEND of mine, who had travelled widely over the world, said to me, "The most fascinating city on the globe is Cairo." If we except the peculiar charm which Jerusalem possesses for every Christian heart, my friend was right in his estimate. I have been nearly a week in Cairo, and the excitement which its novel features produce is almost an intoxication. There are really several Cairos—as there are several nationalities among its 700,000 people. Southwest of this spacious old hotel is the new or "Ismaileeyeh" quarter. This is like Paris, a region of elegant modern residences. Here live the Jewish bankers, the merchants, the Europeans, and some of the rich Pashas. On every Friday afternoon (which is the Mussulman Sabbath) the fine equipages roll in from this quarter, many of them bearing the beautiful Circassian ladies of the Pashas' harems, half veiled, and yet revealing bright eyes and lovely complexions. Before the carriage runs a nimble young Arab footman, in white tunic bound with an embroidered sash, and carrying a staff in his hand. The endurance of these graceful forerunners is wonderful; they will keep out of the way of a pair of horses on a round trot for several miles!

Yesterday afternoon his Royal Highness, the Khedive, drove by with a fine pair of dark bays, and his minister, Zuylfekah Pasha, by his side; behind him rode a half dozen guards in white uniforms. The Khedive looks about thirty, has a fine eye and clear olive complexion, and wore a light overcoat and red tarboosh, or fez cap. Mohammed Tewfik is a less adventurous man than his father, Ismail, who abdicated two years ago; he is more under the control of England and France, who now hold Egypt's purse-strings. The Khedive is a man of good purposes, and I was glad to put my eye on the grandson of the great warrior, Ibraham Pasha, and—the successor of the Pharaohs.

Every morning early, while the air is cool enough at this season for an overcoat, I love to sally off into the old narrow streets of Cairo, around the "Mooske," which look now just as they did in the "Arabian Nights." The streets are about twelve feet wide, some of them only seven or eight. As we pass through, old "Ali Baba" meets us in a white turban, trotting along on a donkey; and "Fatima" steals by us wrapped in a black silk mantle, her eyes peeping out above her veil. A camel comes ambling through the narrow streets, laden with a small stack of green clover; on him rides one of the Fellaheen, or farmers, from the other side of the Nile. Presently a herd of goats push by us, followed by an old man in blue gown and white turban, who sings out a monotonous cry.

He is the milkman on his morning rounds; his customers come to their doors, and he halts and milks for them enough for their day's supply. After him comes the water-carrier, with a goat-skin bag slung over his shoulders, filled with the precious fluid.

Egypt is the joy of us teetotalers, for cold water is king. I have not seen scarcely a dram-shop, and nobody drunk. But water is everywhere—whether it be drawn up by a buffalo in water-wheels and poured over the thirsty fields, or whether it be carried in jars on women's heads, or sprinkled from goat-skin bags through the dusty streets, or whether it be drank eagerly from the beautiful public fountains in the thoroughfares. He is a public benefactor who erects a stately marble fountain to which "whoever is athirst may come and drink the water of life freely." Some of these fountains are so large that in the room above them a small Arab school is held Every drop of water in Egypt comes from yonder Nile. It is rather low to-day, but the annual inundation will begin in June and reach its highest mark in September. Then it will sweep for seven miles across yonder fertile valley, until it reaches to the Pyramids and the Sphinx, and touches the yellow sands of the great Sahara. What a beautiful type of the Gospel is the abounding Nile, for wherever its delicious water does not come, all is left to desert and desolation.

Last Friday I mounted my donkey, "Yankee Doodle Dandy" (though I suspect the little beast bears another name when an Englishman rides him), and my Arab guide, Ali Hassan, took me to see the "Dancing Dervishes." They are a small Persian sect, and their mosque is in the Helmeyeh, a narrow street not far from the Citadel. These singular creatures perform their weekly *whirl* or dance at two o'clock every Friday. I found about twenty-five of them seated around a small circular floor. They wore a tall brown hat—that looked like a flower-pot turned upside down—and long gowns of either brown, green, purple or black. An old sheykh acted as a sort of marshal, and at his signal they arose and began to march around the ring, stopping to make a low bow when they reached the sacred prayer carpet. Presently they threw off their cloaks, stepped out into the ring and began to whirl like tops. Each man stood mainly on his left foot, spread his arms out straight, shut his eyes and spun around at a rate that was perfectly astonishing. This whirl, or waltz, was accompanied by two flutes and a tambourine, in a small upper gallery. I timed them with my watch, and the fellows whirled, without becoming dizzy or dropping from vertigo, for full twelve minutes. While they were spinning, the skirts of their white robes stood out like umbrellas. The whole unique performance lasted about one hour, and the spectators left a small "backsheesh" with the doorkeeper.

After this holy waltz—which is certainly more chaste and innocent than the same performance usually is in an American ballroom—we rode up to the famous Citadel.

This stands on a lofty elevation, and was founded by the renowned old Saladin in the time of the Crusades. The view of Cairo and its minarets, and of the distant Pyramids toward sunset is one of the most ravishing in the world. It is a dream of Oriental poetry—made all the more glorious by the rosy tints of the clear Egyptian sky. Close by the Citadel stands the modern Mosque of Mohammed Ali, which is the pride and boast of all the Moslem realm. A description of this gorgeous mosque with its lofty minarets, its columns and interior walls of alabaster, and its swinging lamps and colored windows is impossible. We entered its sacred precincts—after drawing on some clumsy slippers over our shoes—and enjoyed the study of its marvellous splendor, until we almost expected to see its famous old founder, Mohammed Ali, come out from his tomb in the corner, and bow toward Mecca for his evening devotions. Just outside the walls is the very spot where this old hero—the Napoleon of the present dynasty—slew the Mamelukes in 1811, and established the throne on which his great-grandson, the present Khedive, now sits. He was the greatest man the Orient has produced during the present century, and it is a great pity that the European powers did not allow him to go on until he had overthrown the Sultan and cleared the "unspeakable Turk" out of Europe.

From the Citadel Ali Hassan takes me through the Bazaars which line the narrow picturesque streets of the old quarter of Cairo. O, what a crowd of divers colors and tongues and nations—coal-black Nubians, brown Arabs, black-eyed Jews, red-capped Copts, turbaned Turks, Syrians and Franks, press and surge around us! In one bazaar gold and silver wares are made and sold. In another, slippers of various bright hues. In the Tunis bazaar we came upon a handsome young merchant seated in his stall selling slippers. He wore the most beautiful robes of rich yellow silk—between a canary color and orange—that I have yet seen in Cairo. I told him that if he would come to New York he would draw a thousand ladies around him in ten minutes. He laughed very heartily. Beside some of the dealers, their wives were sitting, closely veiled, but peeping out over their "burkos" and listening to the talk of their husband to his customers.

I am deeply indebted to the kindness of my old friend General Batcheller, formerly of Saratoga, and now the American judge in the "Mixed Court," which is composed of judges appointed by the English, American, French, German, Italian, Dutch, and Russian Governments. This Superior Court sits in the Palace of Justice and takes cognizance of all cases between various nationalities, and of all suits against the Egyptian Government. General B—— speaks very encouragingly of the rapid progress which Egypt is making in introducing political and social reforms. New ideas are pouring in; by and by comes the Gospel!

Yesterday I enjoyed my visit to the Sunday school in the noble building of the American Presbyterian Mission. It made my eyes water to see those bright groups of Coptic and Arab boys and girls—in such clean, tasteful dresses—rise up and repeat, in Arabic, the *International Series* of Lessons. They were reciting the same Scriptures which my own blessed and beloved school in Lafayette Avenue, Brooklyn, would repeat in a few hours—as soon as the Sabbath sun in its course reached our American skies. I made them a brief address, which was interpreted into Arabic, and I came away happy—and homesick, too.

VI.

LAST VIEWS IN EGYPT.

Shepheard's Hotel, Cairo, April 21.

EVERY hour brings some new object of interest in this wonderful city—which is a microcosm of all lands, ages, and civilizations. The camel which has just passed my window is such an one as Moses rode here on the banks of the Nile in the time of the Pharaohs. Before the fine carriage of a Pasha that has just passed ran two lithe Arabs in white tunics, with embroidered sashes around their loins and staves in their hands; just so ran the prophet Elijah before the chariot of King Ahab. Yonder woman, who is carrying a jar of water on her head, is like the woman of Sychar whom our Lord met beside the Samarian well. Nubians, Abyssinians, Greeks, Persians, Jews, and Englishmen mingle in the crowds that pass under city gates built eight hundred years ago.

But a modern gas-lamp shines before this hotel, which is occupied by Britons and Americans. My friend General Batcheller called the other day to take me to the Palace of Justice, in which he occupies a seat on the bench of the High Court, as the representative of America. On our way we walked through the beautiful Ezbekeeyeh Park and public gardens, in which I saw banyan-trees with their limbs sending down new trunks into the soil, and pomegranate-trees, and flowering figs, and flaming flower-beds of crimson and orange hues. The Palace was once occupied by the Khedive, and its rooms are gorgeous with chandeliers, gilding, and rich upholsteries. The court-room was much like that of the Supreme Court at Washington. When we entered, the Italian Judge was presiding, and beside him sat the Holland and Austrian judges and two Egyptians. An interpreter stood before the bench, and the case that was on was brought by a Persian plaintiff. The business was conducted in Arabic. Some veiled women were sitting on the floor in the outer hall, waiting to be called as witnesses; and an Englishman stood by smoking a cigar. Amid such a mixture of nationalities I should hardly have been astonished if a newsboy had come into the vestibule and shouted "'Ere's an extra *Herald*—another fire in Chicago!"

But the ancient predominates—and it is as unchanged as yonder Pyramids and the Sahara. On Monday I mounted my donkey, and with our Consul's "kawass" and Mr. Vandyke rode up to the venerable Mosque el Azhar, which is nine centuries old. In this picturesque old mosque is held the famous Mohammedan University, which contains, on an average, 10,000 students from the whole Orient. It is the Vatican of Moslemism. As the place is accounted too holy to be trodden by shoes, we were obliged to draw on a pair of clumsy slippers; but in the neighboring Mosque el Hassaneyn (in which a portion of the bodies of two of Mahomet's grandsons are buried) we had to walk over the rich rugs in our stockings. The vast floor of the "Azhar" presents a remarkable spectacle. At least two thousand young men, in white turbans and blue gowns were seated on the mats, studying algebra, or the Koran—each man swinging to and fro, and rattling away in Arabic, so that the building hummed like an immense bee-hive. In one part of the mosque persons were praying with their faces toward Mecca. In another part, a professor of theology was lecturing to a group of thirty or forty students gathered around him. Many of these are to be missionaries to the interior of Africa or elsewhere, for the old tree of Islam is not dead either at root or top. I observed in one separate room a class of blind students under instruction. These men will officiate at funerals and repeat the Koran as the procession moves through the streets

Last Sabbath was full of interest to me. At eight o'clock I went over to the noble building of the American Presbyterian Mission to attend the Sabbath-school; the Cairenes are early risers. What a delightful spectacle was that roomful of bright-eyed boys and girls; some of them in dress and complexion looking as if they might belong to that beloved school in Lafayette Avenue. The boys wore their red tarbooshes or fez caps, but the girls sat uncovered. Brother Watson was teaching the whole school, before a blackboard, from the "International Series" of lessons, and Miss Johnson (a teacher from Belmont County, Ohio,) had the especial charge of the girls. I addressed them a few words, but it was not easy to speak through an interpreter; and I confess that the sight of that Sabbath-school, recalling home as it did to me, gave me rather a large "lump in my throat." The main work of our Mission here is to instruct the young, both on the Sabbath and during the week. Our day-schools number over one hundred and fifty scholars. Many of these are children of the Copts, who are an influential class in Egypt; they furnish nearly all the accountants, book-keepers, and post-masters, throughout the kingdom.

I stepped in at half past nine to the Coptic Cathedral, which was well filled with a well-dressed assembly. Up in the double row of galleries the female worshippers were *caged* behind a lattice-work of metal, painted green. I am afraid that there would not be so many costly wardrobes in our Yankee churches if all the finery was hidden behind a brass screen. It was Palm Sunday in the Coptic calendar, and in the church and court in front were hundreds of boys waving palm-branches, and recalling the scene of our Lord's entry into Jerusalem. The service was a mixture of Romish ritual and censer-swinging, and of Protestant preaching. I was very sorry that I was obliged to leave before Mr. Fostaille, the eloquent Coptic priest, mounted the pulpit. He is their most celebrated preacher, and is quite evangelical.

From the Cathedral I hastened back to our Mission building, where Dr. Lansing was preaching to a good congregation in Arabic.

The men and women were separated by a crimson curtain three or four feet high. I was struck with the intelligent countenances of Brother Lansing's auditors; he tells me that one of his church-members (a produce dealer) is an annual contributor of about seven hundred dollars to the Mission and its work! That looms large alongside of the benevolent contributions of our average church-members at home. At eleven o'clock I preached to a congregation which embraced seven different nationalities; a few native converts who understand English being present. The Mission is under the direction of the "United Presbyterians," and uses the Psalms of David in all their services. There is a "Presbytery of Egypt" which embraces four central churches—at Cairo, Alexandria, Mansoora, and Assiout—and forty preaching stations. It numbers about eleven hundred communicants, mostly converts from the Coptic faith. A few Mohammedans have been converted, but the difficulties in reaching and moving the followers of the Prophet of Mecca are as yet very great. Dr. Lansing informs me that the late meeting of their Presbytery, held at Fahyoom, was very pleasant; there were thirteen pastors and eleven elders present. Our polity seems to work very smoothly among these descendants of the very people who were the taskmasters of Israel thirty-seven centuries ago. Presbyterianism is like cold water—good for any latitude.

The weather of Egypt is as peculiar as its landscape and its costumes. For the last five days it has been very cool; when the Khedive drove by our hotel on Sunday afternoon, I observed that he wore an overcoat buttoned up to his chin. The week before our arrival the thermometer—under the south wind or sirocco—stood at 95. The air is exceedingly clear and dry, and reminds me of a California Summer. Gen. Batcheller tells me that he has never known it to rain on more than seventeen days in a whole year! When the rain does come it makes sad work with the mud villages of the Fellaheen; their houses, like a bankrupt "go into liquidation." No need of rain is felt in Egypt while yonder Nile yields its abundant supplies.

Thus far I have not met a single American tourist since I left Liverpool! But I encounter plenty of pleasant Englishmen and Scotchmen. My companions out to the Pyramids and the Sphinx were one of the physicians to the Queen and a bright young artist from London. The drive from Cairo is now over a fine road well lined with acacias. On one side I watched the Fellaheen raising water with the shadoof for their barley and ripening wheat; in a field upon the other side was a large herd of camels grazing. After the many admirable descriptions of the Pyramids and their ascent, I need not add any account of my own. I found only one *new* thing, and that is a lately opened pavement or causeway of solid smooth stone leading from the temple beside the Sphinx up towards the second Pyramid. It may have been the causeway over which the stones were slid up to build the pyramid, or it may have been an inclined street for travel. A nimble Arab offered to climb to the top of the great pyramid of Cheops and descend again in eight minutes, for a franc. The fellow scrambled up the huge stones like a sailor up a mainmast, and won his wager. I was deeply impressed with my first view of these wonderful mountains of solid stone, still more by the mysterious Sphinx, but most of all by the vast, awful Sahara that stretches away to the west. It looked as if it were blasted by the hot breath from the nostrils of the Almighty! One can understand better the terrible imagery of the Hebrew prophets after seeing the Egyptian deserts and the wild desolations of the Sinaitic peninsula.

On Tuesday Dr. Lansing called for a drive to the Museum, where we examined the rich treasures collected from Luxor, Karnak, Tanis, etc., and arranged by the great Egyptologist, the late Mariette Bey. A monument to Mariette has just been erected in front of the Museum. Mummies which once were used for fertilizers, have now become so scarce that it is difficult to secure one for the offer of two hundred dollars.

From the Museum we drove to that wonderful region of antiquity "Old Cairo," which lies three miles from the present city. It was built as an Arab city right after Mahomet's death; but even then an old Roman town stood there, part of which was called "Babylon." It seems quite probable that the Apostle Peter wrote his epistles in that ancient Roman town—or in the part settled by a colony from the Persian Babylon. We rode through the spot where this Babylon stood, and gazed with awe upon the solid Roman bastions which have withstood both the sieges of the Caliph Omar and of time itself. Inside of those walls, O what delicious oddities of antiquity! We threaded our way through streets just six feet wide, with the quaintest balconies almost meeting over our heads. We penetrated into the cellar of an extraordinary little Coptic church, far more than a thousand years old, which was as rude as a barn, and yet contained some exquisite mosaics of marble and mother-of-pearl! On the old reading-desk lay an illuminated prayer-book, written in the days of "Magna Charta." An Arab girl lighted a candle and took us down to a subterranean chapel, and showed us the spot where, it is claimed by the Copts, Joseph and Mary rested during their flight into Egypt. However absurd may be that tradition, it is quite certain that that chapel goes back to the early centuries of Christianity, and is one of the few sacred places yet preserved that may have been occupied by the contemporaries of St. Jerome and Origen. That single church, with its surroundings of queer old fossils of architecture and humanity, was worth a journey to Egypt. In an antique synagogue near by is kept a rare old copy of the Pentateuch, which the Jews claim was transcribed by the hands of Ezra. We hammered long and loud at the gate, but the Jewish custodian was "out"; and so. like our friend Dr. Schaff, we missed a sight of the sacred relic.

From all the manifold marvels of Egypt

it is hard to break away. Cairo divides with Jerusalem and Rome the honor of being the most fascinating city of the globe. One week of diligent research has only made me hungry for more. But to-morrow I must be off to join Dr. Barr and Dr. Stewart at Ismailia, and with them to Jaffa and Jerusalem.

VII.

TO THE HOLY LAND.

Mediterranean Hotel, Jerusalem, April 27.

THE day before I left Cairo, a "khamseen," or hot sirocco, from Ethiopia began to blow, and its breath was the breath of a furnace. It was not unhealthy, but it was egregiously uncomfortable. We came by rail to Zagazig, and there entered the Israelite's land of Goshen. When we reached Rameses—which is generally regarded as the starting point of the children of Israel on their exodus—we found it to be the vanishing point of arable land, and were soon in the desert which reaches to the Suez Canal. Brugsch Bey has published an ingenious argument to prove that Moses started from Tanis, or Zoan, and led the Israelites through the rushes of shallow Lake Menzaleh, instead of the Red Sea. But his argument is not much deeper than the Lake.

At Ismailia, after a scorching ride of six hours, we were glad to take a tiny steamboat, and enjoy a cool sail to Port Said, fifty miles. The canal seems like a straight river of three hundred feet in width and twenty-six in depth; it is a splendid monument to De Lesseps—whom I saw riding through the streets of Cairo like a field-marshal. We met some large ocean-steamers moving at the rate of six miles per hour. At Kantarah we crossed the ancient highway over which Jacob brought his household, Alexander led his Macedonians, and Napoleon his French squadrons. At midnight we ran into Port Said, which is a product of the brain of De Lesseps also. It has about ten thousand inhabitants, large warehouses, and is a dissolute place, abounding in dram-shops and dance-houses. There is an increasing tendency among Mussulmen there and in Jaffa to indulge in strong drink. If Mahomet's followers give up their total abstinence practices, they will surrender their chief virtue. They need a reënactment of "Prohibition."

On Saturday evening we went on board the Austrian Lloyd steamer, and on Sabbath morning caught our first view of the Holy Land. Ancient Joppa—or Jaffa—rises very picturesquely on a bluff, and its suburbs to the south look very attractive from the water. We ran in close to the reef, and soon a swarm of Arab boats was raising a Babel about us. Mr. Clark, an intelligent young American from New Hampshire who now acts as the agent of the Cooks, came out to meet us with his uniformed crew of "Cook's boatmen," and we were soon at the landing where Jonah set off for Tarshish. After a short walk beyond the city walls, we found ourselves nicely fixed in the "Jerusalem Hotel"—surrounded by orange-groves and the neat dwellings of a German colony.

In the afternoon I preached to quite a congregation, in the chapel of the "Mary Baldwin Mission," an American institution for the native children. Miss Arnot, who conducts the celebrated school in Jaffa, was present. After service we walked into town, through groups of women carrying water-jars on their heads, and fair Jewesses who looked like Ruths and Rebekahs, and found our way to the "house of Simon the Tanner." It is an ancient building, close to the sea, and very possibly stands on the site of the original house where Peter lodged. We too went up on the flat roof, and looked away over the Mediterranean, as the apostle looked out over that tranquil sea eighteen centuries ago. The ill-starred ship of Jonah was nowhere in sight—only an Austrian steamer in the offing. All around the roof on which we stood, were families enjoying the evening air, and some of them their evening meal on their housetops.

Early on Monday morning we set off for Jerusalem in two wagons; our party consisting of Doctors Barr and Stewart of Philadelphia, officers of the United Presbyterian Foreign Mission Board, a gentleman from Australia, another from California, and myself. Mr. Clark rode beside us to point out the localities, and he has also rendered us immense service as a guide in Jerusalem. He is well-educated, speaks Arabic fluently, and has the genuine tact of a Yankee. The first half-mile led through orange-groves laden with ripe fruit. Then we came out on the broad, superb Plain of Sharon, which at this season of the year is in all its glory. Behind the cactus hedges were olive-orchards and gardens of figs; far away spread luxuriant crops of barley soon to be ready for the harvest. Scarlet poppies flamed over every field. Along the road we met caravans of pilgrims returning from the Greek Easter festival at Jerusalem —some on foot, and more mounted on camels, horses, and mules. It was a picturesque spectacle and recalled the days when the highways were thronged by Jews going up to Jerusalem to the Passover. One anachronism spoiled the illusion; the whole road was lined, alas! with the *telegraph-poles* of the "Eastern Company"! Only imagine Peter sending a message to Dorcas over the wires!

At Ramleh we halted to ascend the lofty Saracenic tower, and to enjoy the wide view which extends for sixty miles over a stretch of luxuriant verdure, almost equal to that of England. Palm-trees waved their fronds; olive-groves in pale green mingled with the deep hue of the figs and the barley, and the orange-orchards were illuminated with their bright fruit "like lamps in a deep green night." To the northeast arose Mount Ebal. To the south we caught a dim view of Gath and Azotus. Truly it was a land flowing with milk and honey; it was ancient Canaan once more as it kindled the eyes of Caleb and Joshua.

Soon after leaving Ramleh, we crossed the lower end of the valley of Ajalon, above which Joshua commanded the sun to halt in the heavens. Then we entered upon the series of mountains that rise towards Jerusalem, and slowly toiled our way upwards. One beautiful picture on the road I can never forget. It was ancient Kirjath Jearim—where the ark abode for twenty years in the time of David—with its square buildings, its ancient church, a palm-tree rising above its roofs, and a train of camels moving up its narrow street. That was a photograph of thirty centuries ago.

At Kolonieh—which claims to be the original Emmaus—we made our last halt. One more long climb up the rough rocky mountain, a half mile farther on, and lo! the Mosque of Omar rose in sight, and beyond it the green brow of Olivet! Jerusalem was before us. We rolled rapidly through the new suburbs—through a street lined with modern mansions, Russian hospitals, Greek convents, and stately institutions—and then entered the Jaffa gate and were on Mount Zion. Peace be within these walls, and soon the light of Messiah's Gospel upon yonder Olivet once more!

Yesterday was a day of enchantment. We took a walk about Zion; we gazed over at the mountains of Moab; we caught our first view of sacred Gethsemane. We stood by "Robinson's Arch," and strolled among the ruined walls of the old rallying-place of the Knights Templars. We threaded the narrow streets and studied the picturesque crowds that reproduced the days of Solomon and the days of Godfrey of Bouillon. In one respect Jerusalem has suffered great injustice. Most tourists describe it as surrounded by wild, bleak desolation. I expected to see only mountains of glaring white limestone. But these travellers came at the wrong season of the year. April is the Summer of Palestine; although the air yesterday was delightfully cool. As I stood on Mount Zion, the Hill of Evil Counsel and the mountains toward Bethlehem were clothed with verdure. The gardens under Moriah were bright with flowers. Olivet was green, except for the white Jewish tombs on its southern end. Scarlet poppies flamed among the stones of the ancient walls. When we went out of the Damascus gate, and stood on the low hill which many regard as the true site of Calvary, the whole country towards Samaria was luxuriant with waving barley and with olive-orchards. So must it have looked when the blessed Master led his disciples among those very fields, and went towards Galilee. So must the land have smiled when over all its terraced hills and among its rich valleys it supported a population as teeming as the population of Egypt to-day. I thank God that I have seen His goodly land of Canaan—not dreary and desolate as I feared, but arrayed in the bright robes of Summer, and with these everlasting hills wearing a verdant crown of beauty.

VIII.

WALKS ABOUT JERUSALEM.

Mediterranean Hotel, Jerusalem, May 3.

EVER since the days of David, Jerusalem has been a centre for pilgrimage. When on our way up hither from Joppa, we met caravans of Greek pilgrims (returning from the sacred farce of "the fire" on Easter night), some on foot and some on donkeys and camels. On Sunday, at the English Church service, I recognized in the congregation, converted Jews, Arabs from the Bishop's school, Germans, Americans, and Australians; in fact as many nationalities as Peter addressed at Pentecost. Jerusalem is a small city; it has only 25,000 inhabitants, and does not cover as much space as Poughkeepsie; yet all the world flocks thither. There is only one carriage road to it—from Joppa—but if a railway were possible over these rocky heights, the rush hitherward would be prodigious. The common mode of travel in Palestine is either on foot, or on the back of some quadruped; it is difficult to decide which rides the hardest.

During the last week I have taken some delightful and instructive walks about the city and environs, and every foot of ground contains some Scripture history or illustration. My convoy has been Mr. Frank Clark, the conductor for "Thos. Cook & Son"; he has resided in Palestine many years, and speaks Arabic as well as a born Bedawee. My hotel stands on Mount Zion, close by Hezekiah's Pool, and within a few yards of the Tower of David. Starting southward from our hotel door, we soon reach the Armenian Convent, and the building in which the Last Supper is reported to have been celebrated by our Lord with his disciples. This is certainly a fiction; for all Jerusalem has been piled over with the *debris* of twenty sieges since the time when Christ trod the sacred city. Every street he walked through is from twenty to sixty feet below the present surface. There is a Jebusite, a Jewish, a Roman, a Saracenic, and an early Turkish Jerusalem all lying under our feet here to-day. All that is left from the age of our Lord that is now *visible* are a Roman pavement, the lower walls of the Temple, David's Tower, the pools, the rock-tombs, and the glorious, everlasting hills like Olivet, Scopus, and ancient Zion.

Standing on the brow of Zion and looking down toward the valleys of Hinnom or Siloam you see a series of terraces, which are now covered with gardens, barley patches and fig-trees. The rains are over; the cisterns that supply Jerusalem with all its drinking water for the year are filled; the fields are waving for the harvest; and the verdure and foliage are at their best. We wind along outside of the city wall to Mount Moriah, and just under the "Haram," or site of the ancient Temple, we find a path that leads down to the Pool of Siloam. There are two pools that bear this name, but they are really one; for the water from the upper pool (now called "The Virgin's") runs by a subterranean passage to the larger pool below. Dr. Edward Robinson and Capt. Warren both crept through this dark passage for several hundred feet on their hands and knees. I am inclined to think that the real fountain-head of this celebrated water-flow is up near the spot where Pilate's Judgment Hall once stood. When I went down under a Catholic Convent up there, and stood on a remnant of the old "pavement of *Gabbatha*," I found the water rippling audibly in a deep vault beneath us.

The upper pool of Siloam is reached by descending twenty-nine steps. Down at the foot is a small basin—not much bigger than a bath-tub—filled with clear cold water. While we were there, a pilgrim came down the steps, threw off his uttermost garment, and literally "washed in the pool of Siloam." When our Lord commanded a certain blind man to do that same thing, he probably sent him to the lower pool. It is a walled reservoir, fifty-three feet long, eighteen wide and as many in depth. Not much of the stream runs into this reservoir now; but is carried off in a channel alongside. It interested me to watch the Arab women come with their earthern jars on their heads, or their goat-skin bags on their backs and fill them from the stream. One bright-eyed young woman asked me for "backsheesh," and when I shook my head (for the beggary here is indecently disgraceful) she muttered out in Arabic, "May you be struck with blindness!" If she had known what havoc the catarrh had made with my hearing, she certainly would have spared me my eyesight. These Orientals are as profuse in their benediction and their curses as they were in ancient times. Commonly they are polite to strangers; and the Bedawy chieftain who escorted us through the wilderness of Judea last week, was a model of both courtesy and fine horsemanship. As he dashed away on his steed along the shore of the Dead Sea, he presented a vivid picture of the Jethros and the other Sheikhs mentioned in the Old Testament.

From Siloam we go up the valley of Jehoshaphat. To the right stands the tomb of Absalom. We too flung our stone into the heap that surrounds the handsome young scoundrel's grave. We walk along by the banks of the brook Kedron, but it is already dry. During the rainy season it runs brimfull. Col. Wilson, our Consul, tells me that when the Autumn rains begin and the Kedron fills up, the people of Jerusalem throng down there with songs and shouts to welcome the coming of the water. In the Orient water is counted as God's richest blessing. Why should not we in America learn wisdom from these, our ancestors? We go a few rods up Kedron and there before us is a walled enclosure; above the wall we see the tops of two cypresses and a few venerable olive-trees. That enclosed spot is sacred Gethsemane. Down yonder hill-side from that city gate the Man of Sorrows walked, on that awful night to his struggle with the powers of darkness, on this hallowed ground.

I expected to find Gethsemane desolate and neglected. Instead of that I found it in beautiful order—with an elegant inner iron railing, and laid out in tasteful flower-beds. Alongside of the ancient olive-trees —many hundreds of years old—grow a profusion of roses, carnations, marigolds, heliotropes, and many varieties of fragrant plants. The air was loaded with sweet odors; and the courteous gardener (from a neighboring convent) allowed us to pick as many flowers as we chose. This adorning of the scene of my blessed Saviour's agony was grateful to me. Why not? Did he not bear the grief that we might taste the sweetness of the blessing of redemption? I rejoiced to see these fragrant tributes blooming so thick and rich and beautiful, as tokens of the heavenly hopes that have sprung up from Gethsemane's soil once steeped with tears.

From the sacred garden, a travelled road

that has been a thoroughfare for twenty centuries, leads up around the southern shoulder of the Mount of Olives. It is the ancient road to Bethany. Over this very road our Redeemer often walked; over it he was once brought in triumph amid the waving of palm-branches and the shouts of "Hosanna!" There are only two other places in Palestine where we are sure our Lord once set his feet. One of them is beside Jacob's well at Sychar, and the other is the little hill above Nazareth, on which the Nazarenes have always walked every day.

Yesterday morning early I went out "as far as to Bethany." There is a remain of a Roman pavement to prove that this was the ancient pathway. Just before reaching the village—which stands among fig and olive orchards—I turned aside to see three old tombs in the rocks—and many archæologists think that one of them may have been the tomb of Lazarus. They are an hundred rods from the village—a very probable distance. The tomb that is commonly called by the name of Lazarus is right *in* the little village. I took a candle and crept down a steep winding stairway of twenty-five steps and then reached a square cavity that led down three steps farther into a small cave That cave is the traditional tomb where Lazarus laid for four days in the sleep of death. If it be the true spot, then our Lord wrought that mighty miracle at the bottom of a deep pit where only half a dozen persons could have room to stand. My own judgment inclines toward that other spot I had visited a few moments before.

Dear, hallowed Bethany is now a small Arab village of twenty stone houses, so closely packed together that at a distance they look like an old stone fortification. One ruined house is claimed to be the remnant of the dwelling in which Jesus held sweet converse with Mary and Martha and Lazarus. I have no faith in that tradition. But just behind Bethany—toward Jerusalem—rises a beautiful hill, verdant to the summit. It is the south-eastern spur from the Mount of

Olives. I climbed it with reverent awe, for I firmly believe that it was from that hill, or from its sides, that the Lord of glory ascended up to heaven. Superstition has built no "Church of the Ascension" there as it has on the top of Olivet, over against Jerusalem. No relic-mongers haunt it or desecrate it. It stands in its silent beauty above the little village that Jesus loved to visit, and when he led his disciples "out as far as to Bethany," I believe that he led them there. That green elevation may probably have been the last spot of earth which the incarnate Saviour ever trod.

IX.

THE DEAD SEA AND THE JORDAN.

Jerusalem, May 2.

I AM very glad that the grand old Tower of David stands only a few rods from my hotel window. It is a pleasant thing to be often looking at the one remaining structure on which the eye of the Redeemer may have rested: for though this tower was thrown down in the time of the Crusades, yet the lower portion is rebuilt of the same stones. Not far from the Tower is Christ Church, where I was glad to worship yesterday— not in an unknown tongue. Bishop Barclay, the successor of Bishop Gobat, has a good congregation, largely composed of the young people connected with his day-school for the Jews, and another for Arabs outside of the city walls. Most of the converts made thus far come from the Jewish and the Syrian element. Neither here nor in Egypt have over a dozen Mussulmen been converted to Christianity. Bishop Barclay is a genial, earnest "Low Churchman." In my last letter I referred to Kolonieh as the possible site of ancient Emmaus; but the Bishop has given me some most convincing arguments in favor of Kubeibeh, which stands about eight miles northwest of Jerusalem, just beyond Nêby Samwil.

Last Thursday morning I set off with my four companions upon an excursion, which, although it involved hard horseback travel over rough paths and precipitous mountains, and exposures to blazing noon-day heats, yet was abundantly stimulating and delightful. We were under the direction of Mr. Frank Clark, who loaded up a donkey with rations for the journey. We set our faces for the Pools of Solomon—halting a few moments at the tomb of Rachel by the roadside. The small structure was crowded with Jews, some of whom wore phylacteries, and all were wailing, as they wail beside the remnant of the Temple walls. One old woman was weeping and pressing her withered cheek against the tomb with as much distress as if the fair young wife who breathed out her life there forty centuries ago had been her own daughter. We found the enormous Pools of Solomon (the longest of which measures 580 feet in length) were about half filled with pure water. We rode beside the aqueduct that leads from them, all the way to Bethlehem. Down among the bleak and barren hills we saw the deep, fertile vale of Urtas, filled with gardens and fruit-trees. It is cultivated by the European colony planted by Mr. Meshullam. For a half hour we feasted our eyes with the view of beautiful Bethlehem perched on its lofty hill and surrounded by olive-orchards. So many new edifices have been erected for convents and other religious purposes, that Bethlehem has almost a modern look. As we rode through its narrow streets we saw no Ruths, but an ancient Jew in turban, long robe, and flowing beard, quite answered to my idea of Boaz. We rode to the Convent adjoining the Church of the Nativity, where a rather jolly-looking monk furnished us an excellent lunch. He then took us into the venerable church that covers the subterranean chamber in which tradition has always held that our blessed Lord was born. The chamber is probably a remnant of an ancient khan once belonging to the family of Jesse and of King David. I expected to be shocked by a sham mockery when I entered the church, but a feeling of genuine faith in the locality came over me as I descended into the rocky chamber and read, around the silver star, the famous inscription in Latin, "Here Jesus Christ was born of the Virgin Mary." The three-fold argument for the authenticity of this site is drawn from unbroken tradition, from the fact that Bethlehem has never been overthrown in sieges, and from the other fact that the learned St. Jerome (in the fourth century) was so sure of the site that he came and spent his long, laborious life in the cavern close by the birth-spot of our Lord. I entered with deep interest the cave in which this devout scholar meditated and prayed and wrought the Vulgate translation of God's Word. My visit to the Church of the Nativity was tenfold more satisfactory than that to the Church of the Holy Sepulchre in this city.

At two o'clock, under a broiling sun, our cavalcade of ten horses and mules filed out of Bethlehem and headed for the wilderness of Judea—one of the dreariest wildernesses on the globe. At the head of our line rode the gallant Bedawy chief, the Sheikh Resheid, equipped with sword and dagger, and showing the scars of half a dozen wounds. Resheid is the most powerful Sheikh in Judea, and led the escort of the Prince of Wales and Dean Stanley to the Dead Sea and the Jordan. His presence with us for three days afforded us an excellent opportunity to observe the looks and ways of a high-blooded Bedawy; but his protection was quite needless against the few shabby Arabs whom we met in their filthy black tents in the wilderness. For an hour we rode among barley-fields. I noticed how close the grain grew to the path, and how easy it was for the sower's grain to "fall on the highway." I also saw several plats of angry thorns, which would "choke" any seed which may fall among them.

Our afternoon's march over the bleak, treeless, and brown mountains of the wilderness was inexpressibly tiresome until we came in sight of the Dead Sea. It lay two thousand feet below us—a mirror of silver, set among the violet mountains of Moab. More precipitous descents over rocks and sand brought us, by sundown, to the two towers of the most unique monastery on the globe. The famous Convent of *Mar Saba* is worth a journey to Palestine. For thirteen centuries that wonderful structure has hung against the walls of the deep, awful gorge of the Kedron. It is a colossal swallows' nest of stone, built to the height of three hundred feet against the precipice, and in habited by sixty monks of the Greek Church —genuine Manicheans, and followers of St Saba and St. John of Damascus. No woman's foot has ever entered the convent's walls! Instead of woman's society they make love to the birds, who come and feed off the monks' hands. Every evening they toss bread down to the wild jackals in the gorge below. At sunset I climbed over the extraordinary building—was shown into the rather handsome church, and into the chapel or cave of St. Nicholas, which contains the ghastly skulls of the monks who were slaughtered by Chosroes and his Persian soldiers —and gazed down into the awful ravine beneath the convent walls. Some monks in black gowns were perched as watchmen on the lofty towers; others wandered over the stone pavements in a sort of aimless vacuity. What an attempt to *live* in an exhausted receiver!

The monks gave us hospitable welcome, sold us canes and woodwork, and furnished us lodgings on the divans of two large stone parlors. One of the religious duties of the brotherhood is to keep vigils, and through the night bells were ringing and clanging to call them in to their devotions. The vermin in the lodging-rooms had learned to keep up their vigils also; and as the result our party —with one exception—had a sleepless night. I have such a talent for sleeping, and like Pat "pay attintion to it" so closely, that I was able to defy even the fleas and mosquitoes of Mar Saba. By daylight the next morning we heard the great iron door of the convent clang behind us like the gate of Bunyan's "Doubting Castle," and for five hours we made a toilsome descent of the desolate cliffs to the shore of the Dead Sea. That much-maligned sea has a weird and wonderful beauty. We took a bath in its cool, clear waters, and detected no difference from a bath at Coney Island except that the water has such density that we floated on it like pine shingles. No fish from the salt ocean can live in it; but it is very attractive to the eye on a hot noon-day. A scorching ride we had across the barren plain to the sacred Jordan—which disappointed me sadly. At the places where the Israelites crossed and our Lord was baptized it is about one hundred and twenty feet wide; it flows rapidly and in a turbid current of light stone color. In size and appearance it is the perfect counterpart of the Muskingum a few miles above Zanesville. Its useless waters ought to be turned off to irrigate its barren valley, which might be changed into a garden. For beauty the Jordan will not compare with Elijah's Brook Cherith, whose bright, sparkling stream went flowing past our lodging-place at Jericho. We lodged over night in a Greek convent (very small), and rode next morning to see the ruins of the town made famous by Joshua, Elijah, Zaccheus, and the restoration of Bartimeus to sight. Squalid Arabs haunt the sacred spot.

Our climb from Jericho to Jerusalem was hot and toilsome—past the wild gorge of the Brook Cherith, and up rocky ravines, till we reached the fountain of En Shemesh. There we halted at a ruined khan, and I was glad to throw myself on the ground, utterly tired out. While we rested and lunched on eggs and oranges, the Sheikh Resheid amused himself playing cards with a brother Arab. Our last march brought us up among the olives and fig-trees of dear, blessed Bethany! I could have kissed the very ground. Its soil is hallowed with the footsteps and the tears of the Man of Sorrows. So ended our delightful journey.

Every day here is wonderful; I seem to be in an enchanted dream. A few nights ago I went out on the flat roof of our hotel near midnight. Jerusalem was silent and dark except where a lamp gleamed here and there in a window. Before me lay Olivet with its outline barely discernible in the dim starlight. Beneath it was Gethsemane: and not far from me is the reputed site of Calvary. I began to recall the scenes of that memorable night when Jesus went out of these streets to his betrayal. I repeated to myself those lines my dear Lafayette avenue flock love to sing:

> " 'Tis midnight; and on Olive's brow
> The suffering Saviour weeps alone."

So actual, so near, so vivid, did the scenes of the Last Night rise before me, that I was perfectly overpowered. That one hour was a sufficient reward for all my long journey to the world's only Jerusalem.

X.

THE OLD AND THE NEW.

Jerusalem, May 6.

"JAPHET shall dwell in the tents of Shem" is a prediction that finds fresh illustration now in the Europeanizing of the Orient. The new patches begin to show in the old garment. As I have already remarked, Egypt is on the "up grade"—and the most intelligent people in Palestine and Syria sigh for a government as endurable as that of the Khedive.

In Jerusalem and Bethlehem I see evident tokens of a new era. If "Japhet" is not here in large numbers, his ideas are coming in a steady stream. To be sure, Palestine *in the main* is the Palestine of ancient days. There is not a newspaper published in the whole land, for the two petty sheets issued by the rabbis here do not deserve that name.

There is only one carriage-road, and that leads from Jerusalem to Jaffa. A railway is no more to be thought of over these precipitous hills than an orange-tree in Greenland. Across the beautiful and fertile plain of Sharon I saw the "fellaheen" driving the same clumsy plough that was driven by the prophet Elisha. The Arab women at Jericho sat grinding at the mill, after the fashion of their ancestors. All Palestine rides yet on camels and on the "foal of an ass," as in the time of our Lord; but still the tokens of change are in the air. A post-office (managed by Austrians) will carry this letter to the ancient Joppa of Jonah and of Dorcas, and place it on board of an Austrian mail-steamer. There is a new Jerusalem springing up rapidly outside of the old city walls, toward the west. For a half mile the street is lined with handsome buildings—some of them schools, hospitals, and convents; some of them quite elegant residences of merchants and bankers. The Anglican bishop, Dr. Barclay, tells me that not one of these edifices was standing when he came here nineteen years ago. Jerusalem has absolutely grown more during that time than some of the towns in the interior of New York.

Along the turnpike to Jaffa runs the telegraph wire, and on the plain of Sharon stands the large "Jewish Agricultural College," surrounded by a model farm and thrifty nurseries. Bethlehem is a thriving town—largely it is nominally Christian—and it carries on extensive manufactures in mother-of-pearl. The Bethlehemites brought back from our Centennial Exhibition at Philadelphia about seventy thousand dollars as the net profit of the sale of their beautiful wares. If Palestine were only delivered from the tyranny of the Sultan, or were ruled by such a man as the Pasha Roulff (the Governor of Jerusalem), it would rise rapidly into a new era of economic progress. The Sultan's touch and tread are *death*.

Last Monday I walked up the Valley of Hinnom, the ancient "Gehenna" of the days of Moloch. I expected to find a horrible desolation; but, instead of that, I found a valley full of olive orchards, and on its slopes toward the Hill of Evil Counsel I saw new buildings, and among them were several built by the legacy of Judah Touro, the American Jew. However dismal Gehenna may once have been, it is now a far better type of Paradise than of Purgatory. Yesterday Bishop Barclay called to take me out to the anniversary meeting of the "Talitha Cumi," an admirable institution for Arab girls, built and controlled by the German deaconesses of Kaiserwerth. The good Bishop wore his canonical hat and knee-breeches, and was preceded by two Arab guards, armed with swords and staves; and the motley crowd of Arabs, Jews, Armenians, and Syrians politely saluted us as we passed. I wish, by the way, that our Yankee nation would pick up some lessons in courtesy from these Orientals, whom we count "heathen." When I happened to look in upon some Jewish schools, the little fellows, who were sitting cross-legged upon their mats, all jumped up instinctively and remained standing until I motioned them to their seats. At Cairo the Arab chamberman came into my room and said "Good night," in the most homelike way, every evening. Blessings on the fellow! He almost seemed like one of my family. When I was down in the Wilderness of Judea, the gallant Bedawy chief, Sheikh Resheid, who escorted us, had the courteous bearing of a native prince.

But to the "Talitha Cumi." We found a handsome stone edifice out on the Jaffa road, with a garden in front, well stocked with figs, pomegranates, and vines, mingled with our hollyhocks and roses. The institution is managed by a company of German deaconesses, who were attired in blue gowns and jaunty white caps. In the three rooms opening into the central hall were gathered more than an hundred bright-eyed Arab girls, dressed in European style. How sweetly they sang the old German hymns in "plain song"! Baron Munchausen the German Consul, and a banker made speeches; the English bishop presided; a report was read; and everything done quite in our own style, even to the passing around of refreshments afterward. I could almost imagine that I was attending the anniversary of my own "Olivet Mission," in Brooklyn. The Deaconesses have also a well-managed hospital near this hotel.

Here in Jerusalem we have no American mission. The chief work done in English is by the London Society for the Jews. They have a handsome church on Mount Zion; and a neat chapel, in which I made a missionary talk, last evening, to a good audience, composed of converted Jews and English residents and visitors. There is a prodigious difficulty in moving the Jews in Jerusalem; first because those who live in the city of their fathers are intensely bigoted in their faith, and secondly because so many of the Jews here live entirely on the pecuniary bounty of their rich brethren in Europe. Then, too, if a young Jew turns Christian, he finds no employment among his people here, and often has to emigrate. But in spite of these difficulties, a considerable number of Jews have been received into the membership of "Christ Church," under the oversight of the Anglican bishop. The Bergheims (bankers), Conrad Shick the antiquarian architect and Mr. Sapphira are all proselytes from Judaism. I was much interested in visiting the hospital and the schools conducted by the London Society. In the girls' school I observed that the room appropriated to day-scholars was empty. The reason assigned was that the Jews of Amsterdam had remonstrated with the parents of the children and persuaded them to take their children from the Christian school and place them in one of their own. An additional backsheesh in the shape of a daily breakfast and dinner is offered to every child of Israel who will return to the schools of the Rabbis. "We will get them all back again," said the English teacher to me; but by what methods she did not explain. Labor to convert the Israelites is like the road from

Jericho and the Jordan—rather hard and up-hill.

The Jews compose about one third of the population of the city. They live chiefly upon Mount Zion, and whether they have come thither from Germany, or Poland, or Russia, or Holland, they are always and everywhere the "peculiar people." Their Judaism is as essentially a part and parcel of them as their keen eyes and their aquiline noses. It is on account of their intense attachment to the faith of their fathers that they have come to live and to die in the Holy City. A large portion of them are supported by the bounty of Sir Moses Montefiore, and other wealthy Jews in Europe; it may be imagined therefore how seriously this fact impedes all efforts to convert them to Christianity. A Jew in Jerusalem is not much more impressible than a Mussulman in Mecca. It has only been after the most untiring labors that Bishop Barclay, Mr. Kelk, Mr. Friedlander, and the other missionaries of the London Society have succeeded, during twenty years, in gathering about sixscore of proselytes into "Christ Church."

I looked into the chief synagogue on Mount Zion the other day. About a dozen gray-bearded Israelites were studying the Talmud. Some looked like Abraham—and some like Shylock. In about such an edifice our Lord stood up to expound the prophecies of Isaiah at Nazareth. As I was passing through the Jewish quarter I heard the hum of children's voices, and went into one of the principal schools. Upon the floor and upon low seats were a crowd of boys sitting cross-legged, swinging back and forth, and all repeating something that sounded like "Alah-alah-lah-lah-lah" in a rapid roll. Their teacher was smoking a cigarette and kept up as steady a chatter as his pupils. In some rooms they were studying the Pentateuch; in others they were busy over their arithmetics. Their school-books were well printed.

I am never weary of studying the everyday life of the dwellers in Jerusalem. Every color, kind, and costume are represented in the streets. The streets themselves are about as wide as the hall of an average house in America—except "David" and "Christian" streets, which reach the remarkable width of about fourteen or fifteen feet. In these two thoroughfares a few dim lamps are hung at night; in all the other alleys the few persons who venture out at night carry their own lanterns. Many of the streets are arched over with heavy stone, and look like long vaults. Through these streets pours a steady stream of foot-passengers, camels, and donkeys, so thick and confused that one must walk circumspectly or he will be run over. As to the filth of these thoroughfares, it is so amazing as to even make New York seem clean in the comparison. One excuse for this chronic nastiness is the scarcity of water; for all that the inhabitants have to rely upon is the rain water which falls during about three months, and is preserved in cisterns for use during all the rest of the year. Into the sides of these narrow streets are let a series of rooms (or caves) about ten feet square which constitute the shops and stores of the metropolis of Judea. In one room works a blacksmith with an anvil and an iron vice like ours. In the next shop a closely veiled Arabic woman is buying a silk dress; there is only space for the salesman and about six customers. Next to the dry-goods shop is a grain market with heaps of wheat, sesame, rice, and barley on the floor. A woman is filling a half-bushel with barley and squeezing it down with her hands so that she may furnish "full measure, *pressed down*, and running over." So does every little act throw light on Scripture in this land of the Bible.

Next to the grain-market is an ancient khan, on whose seats are a group of country folk, some smoking their narguilèhs and some fast asleep. These Orientals lie about, fast asleep, in the mosques, in the streets, on a camel's back, or anywhere. Behind the seats in the khan are a dozen donkeys being fed on barley-straw. It must have been in the subterranean room of just such a khan at Bethlehem that our blessed Lord was born. Probably the khan at Bethlehem belonged to the descendants of David, so that Jesus was born on the actual spot where Ruth, Jesse, and the Psalmist had once resided. Next to the khan we come to a shop in which a cotton-dresser with a clumsy instrument like an one-stringed harp, is dressing raw cotton from Egypt. Next to him is a money-changer and he is probably a Jew. Along through the crowded streets push and press a motley throng of Jewesses with white cotton mantles over their heads—of bare-legged Arabs—of Armenian priests with slouching black hoods—of Greek priests with caps like a section of a stovepipe—of Franciscan friars in gray robes with a rope tied around their waists—of turbaned Turks and occasionally a Bedawin chieftain from the desert. I saw one splendid looking fellow to-day well mounted, and carrying a spear twelve feet long. Occasionally we meet an Arab woman bearing a bag on her back hung by a cord across her forehead. Out of the bag peeps a baby Ishmaelite six or eight months old. The Jewish women and the fellaheen generally go unveiled. The Turkish and the Arabs too of the higher castes wear a thin guaze veil.

Every visitor to Palestine is tempted to try a little identification of ancient sites, on his own hook. I too have caught the infection, and have reached a comfortable degree of assurance on the following disputed points. First, I believe in the genuineness of the Bethlehem Chapel of the Nativity as the true site of the birth of the infant Saviour. Secondly, I believe that the grave of Lazarus was one of the four or five open hewn tombs just out of Bethany—and that our Lord ascended to heaven from that green hill immediately behind Bethany, and not from the summit of Olivet. Thirdly, I do not believe at all in the Church of the Holy Sepulchre as the spot of the crucifixion or of the burial. Nor have I found any intelligent antiquarian here (except my good friend the American Consul) who still holds to that fast vanishing opinion. We shall probably never *know* just where our blessed Lord endured his last agony, or where he was laid with the rich in his death. It may have been the purpose of the All-Wise God to conceal this locality from human knowledge just as the place of the sepulture of Moses has been concealed from after generations.

But among all the sites of the crucifixion that have yet been suggested I believe that the strongest *probability* attaches to that elevation, a few rods northeast of the Damascus gate. It is precisely in the form of a human skull, and in that respect answers to the name of "Calvary." It is a rounded knoll of two or three hundred feet in length entirely bare of trees, and a considerable portion of it is now used as a Mohammedan burial-ground. Just beyond it, on the road towards Samaria, are the remains of the great Jewish cemetery of ancient times. The Jews —(according to Dr. Chaplin a most acute archæologist) "still point out that knoll by the name of Beth-has-Sekilah or the 'place of stoning,' and state that it was the ancient place of public executions." If this be so, then it is probable that Stephen may have suffered martyrdom on the very spot where his Lord was crucified. That knoll is far enough away from Pilate's Judgment Hall and far enough away, from Mounts Zion, Moriah and Acra to have been outside of the second wall. (If the second wall was *inside* of the spot where the Church of the Holy Sepulchre now stands, then ancient Jerusalem must have been a most diminutive specimen of a city—really not more than a village). No one spot yet suggested as the scene of the last Passion, seems to my mind, to possess such strong arguments in its favor as this spot outside of the Damascus gate. It contains, on its south side, a deep excavation called "Jeremiah's Grotto." From the top, a wide view of Jerusalem and Olivet and the distant hills of Moab is obtained; if our Lord were crucified there, a vast multitude of people could have witnessed the awful spectacle. During my stay in Jerusalem I have gone out, several times, to this bare rounded elevation, and have felt a shudder of awe steal over me at the thought that I might be actually standing on the rocky mound which witnessed the scene of the world's Redemption!

Canon Tristram has lately returned from an exploration of the land of Moab; and Lieutenant C. R. Condor is soon expected here on his way to the survey of the eastern side of Jordan. Since such valuable discoveries have been made by the excavations of Troy, and Mycene, the question may be asked—why are not more thorough excavations made in Jerusalem? To this we may reply that Jerusalem is not a desolate ruin, but a thickly inhabited city. Almost every square rod is covered with solid stone structures—which could only be removed at great expense. The inhabitants are opposed to being dug up and overturned. Skilled labor to carry on such work is very scarce. No extensive and thorough excavations can be made in Jerusalem without involving enormous expenditure of labor and of money. The secret treasures of history and archæology that are hidden beneath the stone foundations of the Holy City are likely to remain hidden for a long time to come.

Great as are the physical difficulties in the way of exploring subterranean Jerusalem, they are not one tittle as formidable as the obstacles to the fulfilment of the devout dream of the "return of the Jews to Palestine." In ancient times the Israelites were an agricultural and herd-raising people. In our day their descendants, scattered over Europe and America, are almost entirely a commercial people. The few Jews who migrate hither are mostly averse to farming. If they cannot aspire to be bankers or merchants, they are content to "dicker" in a small way as hucksters, and petty traffickers. Palestine is a diminutive country, unable at present to maintain any considerable percentage of the Jews now swarming over the world. It is only one hundred and sixty miles long, and at its widest point only fifty-eight miles in breadth.

A large portion of it is wild and desolate rocky hills that can only be made valuable by a costly restoration of the ancient system of irrigation by pools and artificial cisterns. The fertile and arable regions that I have been enjoying in their vernal beauty—such as the plain of Sharon, and the regions about Bethlehem and towards Samaria—are the property of the native "fellaheen," or farmers. They can be dislodged only by purchase, and there is no disposition manifested by Jews to buy them out. The average Jew is more inclined to invest in stocks or jewelry than he is to try "real estate" in Judea. Even if the whole land were now adapted to agriculture and herd-raising, the security of a strong and just government is indispensable to the success of any extensive colonization. The valley of the lower Jordan—now so desolate— might be transformed to-morrow into a fruitful garden, simply by turning the waters of the Jordan over it and putting in the plough. But what colonists will undertake all that labor as long as the Bedawin could swoop down and carry off the whole crop in a single night? Such are some of the hard facts that the believers in the immediate restoration of Israel to Palestine have to encounter. I see no signs of such a restoration. I do not pretend to unravel prophecy, or to limit the wonder-working power of God; but at present there is no more probability of a Jewish occupation of the Holy Land than there is that the Pope will set up his throne in Washington, or that the "Church of the Latter-day Saints" will get possession of Westminster Abbey.

XI.

BEYROUT AND THE SYRIAN MISSIONS.

Steamer "Espero" May 13.

IF it was not easy to leave Cairo, I was still more reluctant to leave Jerusalem. The accomplished Anglican Bishop Barclay, our Consul, Col. Wilson, and other friends were very helpful to me in studying that fascinating ground of prophets and apostles, and of Him who was above them all. I desired greatly to go north into Galilee, but the increasing heat of the weather added to several other strong reasons decided me to return to Jaffa. I had already seen the *representative* places. After traversing the plain of Sharon it was not so important to see the plain of Esdraelon; the view of Bethlehem had to compensate me for not seeing Nazareth; and, aside from its tender associations, the lake of Genesareth does not compare in picturesqueness with the Dead Sea and the mountains of Moab.

On Friday morning, I stowed myself away in a wagon, with three Armenian pilgrims— and an indefinite amount of their bed-quilts and bundles,—and started for Jaffa. In spite of the heat the ride was full of enjoyment; we stopped twice for rest and refreshment, so that our time spent in the wagon was only eight hours. The turnpike is very fair; we passed several lines of camels laden with goods for Jerusalem, and on the back of one I espied a box labelled "Pratt's Astral oil." It was pleasant for me to observe how Brooklyn is shedding light into Judea. The village of "Soba" on a lofty height to our left, contests with "Abou Gosch" the right to an identity with ancient Kirjath Jearim. Either one may be the true site, and much may be said for both. I cannot accept the theory that the valley of Elah, in which David had his duel with Goliath, lies about Kolonieh; it must be several miles farther south. At five o'clock we came in sight of Joppa—for it is dearer to us by its scriptural name than by its modern cognomen of Jaffa. That last hour of my ride, among the enchanting orange-groves near the town, gave me the finest oriental picture I have yet seen. The oranges—of which three million a year are produced in those groves—were in their luscious perfection. Fig-trees, brilliant pomegranate-blossoms, and a few stately palms adorned the road-side. Troops of camels, and of travellers in bright varied costumes poured along. Before me arose Joppa on its hilltops, and beside it sparkled the blue Mediterranean; the memory of Dorcas, and of Peter and of Cornelius added new sweetness to the fragrant air. Behind us was the verdant background of Sharon, and the distant mountains about Bethhoron. My last day in Judea was pleasantly passed in exploring the quaint old streets of Joppa and in visiting the admirable school for Arab girls conducted by Miss Arnot.

The next afternoon I left in this Austrian

Lloyd steamer "Espero" which is on the fortnightly line for Beyrout, Smyrna and Constantinople. She is a good boat, and since leaving Beyrout her first cabin has been filled with a refined and social company—largely Americans. Her decks outside of the main cabin, are densely covered with a menagerie of Turks, Syrians, Greeks, Arabs, and all manner of Orientals, who eat, drink and sleep in the open air. Some of them are pilgrims from Jerusalem. Some are devout Mussulmen, and perform their prayer-service on the deck four times a day with a military precision. A line of them kneel together (facing east), bow their heads to the deck together, rise up together, and then prostrate themselves again, while their lips are repeating lines of the Koran. Certainly a Mohammedan is never ashamed to show his colors.

Among the cabin passengers is a beautiful wife of a Turkish Pasha in Constantinople, who has her meals apart with her attendants, but who mingles with the rest of our company on the deck. She is richly apparelled, and wears a white veil—which she opens at the eyes sufficiently to read or write; but her lustrous eyes, rich complexion, and costume look as if they had come out of the canvas of one of Frederick Bridgman's Oriental pictures. The eastern dress is not always "handy" for work, but it is exceedingly graceful and picturesque in its effects.

On the first evening after leaving Joppa, I watched with intense interest the revolving light on Mount Carmel, and early the next morning caught a fine view of glorious Hermon with its diadem of snow. Soon afterwards we began to see a few buildings on a bluff at the base of Lebanon. I knew at once that they must be those buildings which American piety and zeal have reared as the spiritual lighthouses for Syria and the East. I have only taken off my hat in reverence on two occasions since I left home; once was when I entered the gate of Jerusalem, the other time was when our steamer came up abreast of the American College at Beyrut.

The harbor swarmed with small boats pushing out to meet the steamer, and the first person whom I recognized was Dr. Jessup swinging his handkerchief among a crew of Arab boatmen. If I were to say that the man in that boat was the prince of American missionaries, probably no persons would respond "amen" more promptly than his brethren in the foreign work. In ten minutes we were on shore, climbing the hill to Brother Jessup's residence. But no; we could not go to his house until we had been to see the handsome church in which he preaches, and where, last Sunday, he administered the sacrament of the Lord's Supper to two hundred communicants. Then we must go into the new Sunday-school building erected by Mr. Dale as a memorial of a beloved child gone home to God. It is a gem; and when it is resounding with three hundred and sixty voices singing Christ's praises in Arabic, that room is worth a journey to Syria to see. One other building must be visited, and that was the Printing House which turns out Arabic Bibles and Catechisms, and school-books and tracts and the vivacious newspapers edited by Dr. Eddy. Among the publications issued are "Twelve Sermons by D. L. Moody." So charmed was one of the Greek priests in Beyrout with Brother Moody's discourses that he preached six of them to his own congregation, and the congregation were as much delighted with them as the preacher! Since that performance, the priest has gained a great reputation for originality and eloquence.

Not far from the press-rooms is that little upper-chamber in which Dr. Vandyke translated God's Word into Arabic. Only a few days previously I had stood in the cavern at Bethlehem in which St. Jerome had made the translation of the Latin Vulgate. In comparing the two places, "the glory of the latter house excelleth." Dr. Vandyke himself is now not only a Professor of Medicine in the College, but of Astronomy also. I found the cheery old man in his observatory, busy with his telescope. I said to him—"Well, Doctor, you may study the stars with this instrument, but you have given the Arabic-speaking nations a telescope that reaches into the heaven of heavens."

The main College building stands on a height as commanding as "Pardee Hall" at Easton, Pennsylvania. In its reception-room hang the portraits of William A. Booth, William E. Dodge, S. B. Chittenden, and Dr. Post. These noble men are the Trustees of this noble institution. Adjoining the main building is another erected by the munificence of Mr. Frederick Marquand. If my venerable friend could see that structure before he "goes up higher" he would be more sure than ever before that no investments pay such dividends as money consecrated to the Lord. The Medical College, with its fine lecture-rooms and apparatus, stands a little farther to the east. Dr. Post is busy in preparing a great work on the *Flora* of the

Levant—a region that abounds in rare trees and flowers. My first visit to the College so delighted me that I went up again at five o'clock to attend the evening prayers. The one hundred and twenty students who were present reminded me of a similar gathering in old Princeton—except for the brown complexions and the red fez caps. They sang "Hold the Fort" in Arabic, and one of the Faculty read the Scriptures and offered a prayer. I ventured on a brief speech to the bright fellows (some of whom have such names as "Amin Abdallah" and "Rashid Haddad"), and I never had a more enthusiastic audience. There is only one Mussulman now in the College, but there would be many scores if the Faculty would consent to omit direct religious instruction; this they have wisely and firmly refused to do. At Dr. Jessup's table I had the privilege of meeting President Bliss, and the Professors, with several other friends. That American reunion with these beloved brethren—where every dish on the table tasted of *home*—gave me the happiest hour I have passed in the Orient.

Great as is the work being done by the College it does not surpass that which is being wrought by the Female Seminary—in charge of Miss Jackson and her associates—which contains about one hundred and fifty pupils. A large number of them sang for me "Wonderful Words of Love." In the room I observed a Syrian orphan-girl who is supported by five young girls in my own Sabbath-school—which has also furnished one of the volumes for the Sabbath-schools of Syria. The Seminary charges a moderate tuition-fee for most of its pupils, and wisely too, for what costs nothing is held at too small a value. Other denominations beside our own are at work in Beyrout. The "British Syrian Schools" have nearly three thousand scholars in the whole country; while those under American control have four thousand two hundred and fifty scholars. The German Deaconesses of Kaiserwerth are providing for many orphans; Miss Taylor has about fifty Moslem girls under her instruction; and the Jesuits have an imposing structure into which they decoy as many as possible. The Greek Catholics are "running an opposition" to the Jesuits.

With a reverent gratitude I went into the Protestant Cemetery and stood beside the graves of Pliny Fisk and Dr. Eli Smith, the founders of this glorious Syrian Mission. The mustard-tree they planted has waxed strong and broad. To-day it can point to thirty-three missionaries, one hundred and fifty native laborers, nine hundred communicants, seventy-three preaching stations, one hundred schools, and four thousand two hundred and fifty scholars—with a College that will make itself felt over the whole Orient. Who that reads such inspiring facts will not resolve to double his contributions to Foreign Missions?

I longed to spend more time at beautiful Beyrout and to climb the sides of Lebanon which are sprinkled thick with villages. But no other steamer will leave for Constantinople in a fortnight, and I do not wish to miss the annual gathering of the missionaries that takes place next week on the Bosphorus At the hour of sunset—when the blue Mediterranean was burning with a crimson glow— we waved our adieux to Doctors Bliss and Jessup, and took our last look at those sacred buildings which " fling afar the sweet smell of Lebanon."

XII.

CHIO—AND A VISIT TO EPHESUS.

Steamer "Espero" May 14.

ON the evening of Monday our good steamer sailed out of the harbor of beautiful Beyrout, with the setting sun kindling the peaks of Lebanon. Jerusalem means the past; Beyrout is the harbinger of a new day for Syria and the Levant. Its population has risen rapidly from thirty thousand to eighty thousand; already it is the centre of Christian influence in the Orient. When the American Board turned over that Mission on Mount Lebanon to the Presbyterian Church they gave us their crownjewel.

We laid one day at Cyprus, the scene of the first foreign mission ever undertaken by the apostles. Both the places in which Paul labored are now in ruins. I had hoped to get a good view of Patmos, but our steamer was behind time, and we passed it in the evening. By moonlight I saw only its dim shadowy outlines; like the wonderful Apocalypse that was there revealed to the apostle John, it was overhung with solemn mystery. But on no spot outside of Jerusalem have I gazed with such a thrill as upon that lonely isle.

Our steamer, loitering leisurely along over the most fascinating sea on the globe, requires seven days to go from Beyrout to Constantinople. On Friday morning at daylight we were off the ill-fated island of *Scio* —or "Chios," as it is called in the Acts of the Apostles. Our Captain kindly consented to land for an hour, in order to allow the passengers to examine the ruins of the recent terrible earthquake. Certainly no place has been the scene of such calamities during this century as the historic island of Chio. In 1822 the Turks brutally massacred or carried into bondage forty thousand of its inhabitants. Only a handful were left. As soon as the island had become re-peopled and revived, an earthquake overthrew a large portion of its chief city. A few weeks ago came the third great calamity, which has excited such deep sympathy over the civilized world.

The City of Scio lies close to the sea, at the base of a steep range of volcanic mountains. As we drew up into the harbor, we could see, from the ship's deck, the desolation on the shore, extending even to the half-dozen neighboring villages. Arriving at the wharf, such a scene of havoc and of horror presented itself as I have never beheld! The market-place or square near the landing was covered with tents, in which the relief committees and some of the surviving citizens were quartered. I saw two persons dressing themselves who had slept during the night on a pile of lumber. We walked through several streets that were heaped up with ruins to the depth of six feet! Every house on both sides was a mass of mingled walls, rooms and roofs thrown into the wildest confusion; pieces of furniture were still protruding from beneath chamber floors, and rafters were thrust out from the depths of cellars. Not a living creature was visible in a whole block that two months ago teemed with happy occupants. One minaret of a mosque was standing, while the buildings beside it were hurled into ruin. As far as I could judge, about half of the city is destroyed—or so shattered that a large expenditure will be required to restore them. Large numbers of dead bodies still lie buried under the *debris*. How or why poor Scio is to be rebuilt I cannot conceive. It would seem to be the height of hazardous folly to attempt to perpetuate a town which has suffered such calamities and is exposed to a repetition of earthquakes in all time to come.

At noon of the same day we entered the superb bay of Smyrna—a city that is famous in the past as being the seat of one of the "Seven Churches of Asia," but is now a busy commercial city, half European and half Asiatic. A less interesting city I never entered; for beyond the tomb of the martyr Polycarp

CHIO—AND A VISIT TO EPHESUS. 143

there is not one relic of the past worth looking at. I did indeed see with great satisfaction a small mission-room for sailors on the quay, which bears the name of the "Seamen's Rest," and is well stocked with newspapers, Bibles and Scripture-texts hung upon the walls. Some Christ-loving hearts have opened this safe harbor for tempted sailors in the midst of drinking saloons and tobacco shops.

But if Smyrna is totally devoid of interest to anybody but a drug-merchant or a dealer in figs and fruits, there is a spot fifty miles from it that stands *next to Jerusalem* in the eyes of all students of the New Testament. Jerusalem is first, and then comes EPHESUS. For five centuries it was one of the most superb cities of the Orient. Alexander the Great visited it, and sat for his portrait to Apelles, who was its chief painter. Xenophon marched through it, and Hannibal there met Antiochus. Cicero was entertained by its polished citizens, and Antony and Cleopatra held their voluptuous revels there.

Close by its walls stood one of the seven wonders of the world—the magnificent Temple of Diana. Around no one city outside of Judea are the names of the apostles Paul and John so closely entwined as about that city to which Paul addressed that Epistle that will be read while humanity endures.

Several of my fellow passengers were as keen as myself for a visit to Ephesus. It lies about fifty miles from Smyrna in the valley of Cayster, and on the line of a railway which a British company have constructed to Aidin. The daily train leaves in the morning, and our only chance was to get there during the afternoon after our arrival. So the moment that our steamer had anchored inside of the breakwater, two of our company were despatched to the railway station. The superintendent agreed to furnish to our party of seventeen a special train for one hundred dollars. The bargain was soon struck; a locomotive was ready in a few minutes with three luxurious cars, and we were soon whirling away through the vineyards and mulberry groves that lie southeast of Smyrna. The train made no halt, and in one hour and a half we were at the little Turkish village of Ayasolook.

A half mile from this village lie the ruins of the famous city. We passed a line of broken columns of an aqueduct—on the top of each one of which was perched a stork upon its huge nest of twigs. Then we came to a mosque which had once been a Christian church, and which was largely built of the granite and marbles of ancient Ephesus. A little way beyond in an open field—in a large excavation, lie strewn around the broken fragments of marble Ionic columns. These are everything that is left of the once proud Temple of Diana.

These would never have been discovered —a dozen feet under ground—but for the persistent courage of Mr. Wood, the English antiquary. After long search he found the spot where the mighty edifice once stood that stretched three hundred and fifty feet by one hundred and sixty—a poem in white marble! In its dazzling splendor it may well have aroused the pride of the Ephesians to cry out "great is Diana," and it required no small intrepidity in Paul and Timothy to assail such a citadel of superstition.

A half mile away we came to the massive ruins of the "Stadium"—and beyond them we reached the most intensely interesting spot of all. Every reader of the Scripture narrative will remember how, during the tumult raised by Paul, the people of Ephesus rushed into the "theatre." Not an enclosed building, but a huge amphitheatre walled around, on the side of Mount Prion, and open to the sky. It was to the actual remains of that theatre that our guide conducted us. The seats—that would contain 60,000 spectators—all disappeared centuries ago, but the shape of the theatre and a portion of its rear walls remain. The ruins of its magnificent white marble entrance are still there—some of them beautifully sculptured, and some stones covered by Greek inscriptions. My heart leaped quick when

I thought—here by this vast auditorium the great Apostle once stood! These solid rocks of Mount Prion once echoed to that transcendent voice! Over this hill John has walked, and Timothy and many of those early saints; somewhere near at hand Aquila and Priscilla taught Apollos "the way of God more perfectly." I climbed around the rocky hillside and examined the ruins of the "Odeon," and of the "Gymnasium," and saw the fabled cave of the seven sleepers. Every few steps my feet struck against sculptured marbles lying in the grass. On every side was utter, silent desolation. The ruins of Baalbeck are not more deserted. Yet the whole area was to me instinct with glorious life. It was enough that I was at actual Ephesus—the Ephesus of Paul and Apollos —the Ephesus in which the Beloved Disciple closed his long life, the city to which he sent the inspired message in the Apocalypse!

We walked four miles around and over the ruins of the wonderful city. The moon was already rising over the hills toward

Sardis before we got back to our train. Physically we were weary and hungry, and glad to set our faces toward Smyrna, which we reached at half past nine o'clock. But what were hunger and fatigue—even tenfold greater—when we remembered that we had been at one of the great fountain-heads of divinely inspired thought and action for all coming time? We had been at the very spot where "for the space of three years Paul had ceased not to warn every one, night and day, with tears," for Jesus' sake. We thanked God, and went to bed tired and happy.

XIII.

ON THE BOSPHORUS.

Constantinople, May 20

FROM Smyrna, our Austrian Lloyd vessel, the "Espero," steamed away again, up the Bay, and out into the enchanting Mediterranean. We were as crowded as ever. The old sheikh from Damascus, whose harem was partitioned off by shawls on the saloon-deck, had to crowd his veiled women into smaller compass to make room for some other polygamous households. The menagerie of orientals on the main deck received some new accessions, including a half dozen sheep and lambs waiting to be sacrificed.

Our steamer, just as it entered the Dardanelles, ran close to the Asiatic shore, and we were able to see the heaps of earth thrown up by Dr. Schleimann on the site of "Ilium," the mounds of Achilles and Ajax, and the harbor from which Eneas set sail. Just before reaching Constantinople we passed San Steffano, where the Russian army laid for several days in full view of the city and within an hour's march. "Why did not you go in?" inquired a friend of mine here, of the Russian commander. His answer was, "It was not because we could not go in, or were afraid to go in; but the time had not come to do that."

I do not wonder that the Turk clings as long and as fast as he can to so magnificent a possession. For with its million of inhabitants, its peerless mosques, its palaces, its unrivalled beauty of situation, its prestige and its power, Constantinople wears a more imperial air than any city on this continent. It is the very perfection of semi-barbaric splendor. Yet with all its gorgeous domes and minarets on the heights, and all its huge iron-clads anchored in the "Golden Horn," and all the fine equipages which its Pashas drive through the Rue de Pera, Constantinople is only half civilized.

It has no educated class, no literature, no science, no high tone of honor; the substance of it is semi-barbarism thinly veneered with external courtesy and some modern mechanical improvements. English engineers have come here and built railways for the Sultan. One of them, a subterranean railway leading up the steep hill from the Golden Horn to the heights of Pera, is a blessing to us travellers. It saves us a tiresome climb up through narrow and abominably filthy streets to our hotels. There is also a line of horse-cars running along the water-side clear up to the Sultan's palace at Dalmabatchi.

We landed on Monday morning from the steamer in row-boats. Our boat was approached by a police-boat; we held up our passports and were told to row on. When we reached the custom-house wharf my dragoman unknown to me slipped a franc into the inspector's hand, and (as his eye is about the size of a franc) he passed my valise without opening. A friend of mine, on *leaving* the city, had his baggage examined, and he was obliged to pay a heavy duty on everything he had bought in Constantinople and was carrying homewards! That is a Turk's method of encouraging us foreigners to purchase the showy knicknacks which are for sale here in the celebrated bazaars. After we landed, the trunks of our party were tied together, and one of the athletic Constantinople porters carried the enormous load up the steep hill to our hotel on the Rue de Pera! They are wonderful specimens of muscle. One of them can carry two barrels of flour at a single load; but you must get out of the track of these human pack-horses, or be run down by them, for they claim "the right of way" against all comers.

Some cities grow upon you by a constant revelation of new beauties; others produce their highest impression at first sight. I have hitherto stood up for Edinburgh as unequalled for picturesqueness of situation; but when I saw the Capital of Islam, enthroned on its lofty hills, and crowned with its domes and palaces and minarets, I was ready to admit that, seen from the water, it is the most magnificent city on the globe. Some of the enchantment vanishes after you land; for many of the streets are narrow and filthy, and the city is a rare combination of palace and poverty, of splendor and shabbiness. The famous Mosque of St. Sophia was the first spot towards which I turned my steps, and with its antique grandeurs all of my readers are familiar from scores of descriptions. I was still more impressed by the Mosque of Suleiman the Magnificent—which is the masterpiece of Saracenic architecture. In the same enclosure with this gorgeous Mosque are four Moslem academies, a hospital, a charity-kitchen for the poor, and a school for instruction in medicine.

One of the finest views I have gained was from the heights of Scutari, across the Bosphorus, and above the famous hospital of Florence Nightingale. But I saw something grander there than domes or palaces. Upon those beautiful heights stands our American Female Seminary, or "Home"; and around it reside our faithful missionaries Dr. George W. Wood and the Doctors Bliss and the veteran Dr. Riggs. I spent a night with Brother Wood in his delightful home, surrounded with American faces, American books and American scenes of consecrated toil. Need I confess that a sharp twinge of home-sickness kept me awake that night?

Early the next morning I was out among the flowers, and enjoying the early pink bloom of the "Judas trees," and the view from the balcony of the seminary. The building is new and commodious—a sort of second edition of "Mount Holyoke." About fifty young Armenian, Turkish, Greek, and Bulgarian girls are in the institution, which is under the superintendence of Mrs. Williams. I conducted the service of morning worship in the chapel; and but for the brunette tinge of countenances, I might have supposed that I was addressing a group of "Packer" girls in my own beloved Brooklyn. They understood nearly every word—for the exercises of the Seminary are conducted in English—and a more animated audience I have seldom addressed. Those churches and Sunday-schools in the United States that are contributing to the support of the Scutari "Home" are making a royal investment of their money.

But if my national pride was up when I visited the Home, it was yesterday exalted beyond measure when I went up the Bosphorus to *Robert College.* It stands on a lofty elevation, at about the finest point on the Bosphorus—just where that stream comes the nearest to rivalling our imperial Hudson. Opposite the College stands one of the many palaces of the Sultan flanked by the green "Valley of Sweet Waters"—and just beside the College are the ancient fortresses erected by Mahmoud in 1453. At that point Darius bridged the Bosphorus for his Persian invaders. But my honored friends. the late

Christopher Robert and Dr. Cyrus Hamlin, made a nobler invasion of Turkey when they conceived and constructed this American College to let the daylight into the dungeons of Moslem superstition. The building is imposing without, and a model of convenience within. The Vice-President, Dr. Long, took me through the museum, geological cabinets, recitation-rooms, and dormitories, and then introduced me to over two hundred young men assembled in the large study-hall. Ten nationalities were represented there—Turkish, Greek, Armenian, Jewish, Russian, Syrian, Sclave, and Bulgarian. They reminded me of a crowd of Yale or Princetonians, especially when they began to "demonstrate." I wish I dared to describe the enthusiasm with which these young men received every allusion I made to the "new ideas" which that American College is giving to them, and which they are to scatter through the Orient. I do not wonder that when the Russian army went home three years ago through the Bosphorus the Imperial Guards came out on the decks and gave three rousing cheers for Robert College!

But that noble institution requires and must have more room for its increasing work. It needs a new building for lecture-halls, chapel, and museum, and to have the present building used for study rooms and dormitories. That edifice ought to be erected, by American money, within two years, and when it is completed it should bear the noble and well-won name of HAMLIN HALL. The institution was founded by Christopher Robert's munificence, but it was born in Cyrus Hamlin's brain.

I count it a precious privilege that during my present visit to Constantinople the annual meeting of the American missionaries of Western Turkey is being held—at the "Bible House" in Stamboul, which is our American "Embassy." The Bythinian Evangelical Union, composed of native pastors and teachers, is also in session. I have been listening with deep interest to the reports made by our missionaries of their last year's hard and honest work—from Kharpoot to Constantinople. When they kindly invited me to address them and the Evangelical Union, I felt how much better was their faithful work than any feeble words I could speak in regard to it. This week alone has convinced me of the *solid value* of Foreign Missions.

I am also as strongly convinced that the Sultan is simply a nuisance on European soil. The Turks cherish with superstitious pride the breach in the old wall of Constantinople through which their ancestors marched *in* four hundred and thirty years ago. I will go a great way to see the breach through which they shall march *out*.

The present Sultan resides in the small palace of Yisdil, on the summit of a hill, and surrounded by a superb park that reaches to the water's edge. Every Friday he comes down through this walled enclosure and rides a few steps to a small mosque near the gate. A large crowd gathers weekly to gaze at the caliph of over one hundred millions of Mussulmen; but he is careful to trust himself outside of his own walls for as few moments as possible. I was urged to go and look at the Pope of Islam to-day; but I do not care to brave this raw, chilly air for an hour simply to see an insignificant-looking man ride on horseback an insignificant distance to say his prayers. One of these days the caliphate will cross the Bosphorus and "head" towards the Arabia whence it originally sprung. The doom of Turkish supremacy is near at hand.

There is an increasing party in Asia who wish to oust the Sultan and put an Arabian descendant of Mohammed into the caliphate. Other great changes will come; but the grandest revolution this superb and wicked city will ever see will be when Protestant missionaries begin to proclaim the Gospel of Jesus Christ under the domes of St. Sophia and of "Suleiman." God speed the day!

XIV.

ATHENS.

Hotel Etrangèrs, May 27.

I WAS not sorry to quit Constantinople with its chilly air, filthy streets, and steep hills, for bright, clean, tasteful Athens—with its marvellous memorials of the past, and its cheerful tokens for the future. My stay here has been rendered all the more agreeable by the comforts of this Hotel des Etrangèrs on the Palace Square; it is quite a model in its good appointments and home-like qualities. What a relief also is the riddance from a tribe of guides and importunate hangers-on about the doorways. Athens is a small compact city, and every intelligent visitor can find his own way. The city of the past, whose glorious ruins lie on or south of the Acropolis, is twenty-five *centuries* old; the city of the present, which lies north and east of the Acropolis, is for the most part, about twenty-five *years* old. These new and elegant houses have just a trifle too much of white, cream color and peach-bloom; for, with the glaring white limestone of the pavements, the effect almost blinds the eye. Added to this is an atmosphere as clear as crystal, through which the sun-rays pour down with unhindered brilliancy.

As soon as I had established my quarters at the hotel, I was in a carriage with my friend, Judge Barringer (the colleague of Judge Batcheller in the "International Court" of Egypt), for a drive to Mars' Hill. We climbed up the dozen steps hewn in the solid rocks, the very steps the Apostle must have trod—and found ourselves on that bald mass of rock on which the original Areopagus held its sessions. Standing there, within pistol-shot of the Parthenon, with what telling effect could Paul exclaim, "God that made the world and all things therein, seeing that he is Lord of heaven and earth, dwelleth not in temples made with hands." As the colossal statue of Minerva Promachus was in full view, he could also remind them that the Invisible Jehovah was not to be graven in the images carved by "art and man's device." As there are only three spots in Palestine on which we can feel assured that our Lord ever set his sacred feet, so there are just two on which Paul must have trod; one of them is the rock of Mars' Hill, and the other is the marble pavement of the Portico, through which is the only entrance to the space around the Parthenon. He must certainly have climbed the magnificent avenue of the Propylea which led to the summit of the Acropolis, and from that lofty height—among the masterpieces of Phidias—he must have gazed down upon the city of the Violet Crown in all its flashing splendor.

About the Parthenon and its widowed sister beside it, the Erectheum, I hesitate to add another line. I have visited them at the early dawn, and sat beside them at the sunset; I have gazed at them from Lycabettus, and from the ship's deck at sea, and every fresh view only increased the enchantment. When Pericles had seen the last frieze placed on the Parthenon, and the last exquisite moulding carved around the doorway of the Erectheum, he had seen the consummate perfection of all that man can accomplish in the horizontal styles of architecture. Since that time the world has seen the perpendicular in its perfection in many a Gothic cathedral, but not one new idea has been added to the Doric and the Ionic in three and twenty centuries. That marvellous sense of beauty which the Greeks of that age possessed wrought itself out in everything it touched.

Our American missionary here, the Rev. Mr. Sampson, took me to the old "Ceramicus" near the temple of Theseus, and showed me the tombs and monuments which have been lately excavated. There I saw the actual charred bones preserved in urns, and the family tombs that go back to the era of Plato and Socrates. On one marble tomb a father and mother are taking leave of the little daughter who was buried beneath, and a pet dog is jumping up wistfully against her as if he would detain her from going. Nearly every scene on the monuments represents the farewells of the departed to their kindred; the sculptures all reveal Greek genius. I read one inscription which contains this passage, "My body, my mortal part lies here in the earth, but my immortal part, my soul, is in the keeping of the Great Treasure-keeper." Perhaps the man who composed this epitaph had been one of the listeners to the great Apostle, and had caught some glimpses into the better life beyond. The wonderfully interesting discoveries made by these excavations in the Ceramicus, and also the unearthing of a supposed temple of Esculapius, just beside the Acropolis, prove what valuable treasures are yet buried up all along the Piræus road, and the banks of the Ilissus.

The most prominent residents in Athens now are Dr. Schleimann and his brave and genial Grecian wife; their house, near the Palace, is the most superb in the city. I shall ever remember gratefully their cordial hospitalities, and their enthusiastic talk over the relics of Troy, which they showed to me in a large lower hall of their mansion. The Doctor has just returned from a visit to the Troad, and his indomitable energy will soon be delving among some other buried cities in the Levant. The frescoes on his drawing-room ceiling represent the education of a group of children in digging—until in the last scenes a group of romping cherubs are seen carrying off the relics from the ruins of Mycene. So intensely classical are the good Doctor and his young wife that they have named their two children " Andromache " and " Agamemnon." This reproduction of ancient names all over Athens is sometimes quite startling. For example, the present "Areopagus," a superior City Court, with its fifteen Judges, holds its sessions at the corner of Sophocles and Aristides streets. Every new edifice is so constructed as to preserve the salient features of Greek architecture; and the Greek merchants who now stand at the head of commerce all over the Levant are sending home their wealth to adorn and beautify Athens. The time is at hand when visitors from all lands will come hither to see the city of the present as well as the matchless remains of the city of the past.

From my window every day I see the King George Ist and his popular Queen driving by from their palace, a few rods distant. He has a manly, intelligent face, and she has a sweet countenance and a look of practical and domestic common sense that is very winning. During the late *scare* about a threatened war with Turkey, the Queen joined a company of ladies from the town, in sewing garments for the soldiers. She worked as industriously as the rest of them, and one day, when her sewing-machine broke, she took it up in her arms and carried it out into another room to be mended. Royalty all over Europe is becoming republicanized in dress and demeanor; it is only such half-civilized potentates as the Sultan and the Shah of Persia who affect the old nonsense of personal sacredness. The present king is a brother of the Princess of Wales, and a staunch Protestant. His private chaplain, Rev. Mr. Peterson, is a fervently evangelical man; on the morning of "Ascension Day" I heard him deliver a most eloquent and spiritual discourse in the Chapel of the Palace.

Protestantism is as yet weak in numbers here. The Greek Church is the national religion, and has been offensively bigoted in past years. I have looked into the Metropolitan Cathedral, and found it very difficult to distinguish any real difference between its pomps and pageantries, its candles and crosses and incense, and confessionals, and pictures, and those in any average Popish Mass-house. Romanism and the Greek Church are twin institutions: intelligent Musselmen judge of Christianity from these two, and they, very naturally, conclude that the religion called

Christian is simply a system of idolatry and image-worship. This is the chief hindrance now in reaching the followers of Mohammed with the pure Gospel. They judge of the truth by its counterfeit.

We have a brave little Mission here under the charge of the American Presbyterian Church, *South*. Their missionaries are Mr. and Mrs. Kalopothakes (formerly Miss Kyle) and the Rev. T. R. Sampson, from Norfolk. He is a most scholarly and energetic young minister, the son of the late Dr. Sampson of Virginia. They are assisted by Mr. Antoniades and Mr. Liaoutsi here, and by Mr. Michaelides, who preaches at Volos, and Mr. Egyptiades, who has charge at Thessalonica. A few weeks ago they organized their first Presbytery, and named it "The Presbytery of the Greek Evangelical Church." Here in Athens their place of worship is a plain, neat structure near the Arch of Hadrian. But these brave, earnest workers deserve a new church-edifice in a more central position. I attended the morning service on Sunday; the house was filled by a most intelligent-looking congregation, and the discourse was delivered by one of the native ministers. It seemed primitive and apostolic to hear the Greek Testament read from the pulpit, and when the congregation sang a Greek hymn to the same sweet American air as "What a Friend We have in Jesus," I could not keep back the tears. Blessings on this noble mission under the walls of the Acropolis! Once more the "men of Athens" can hear Paul's gospel-message in Paul's own tongue. The Presbyterians of the United States ought to give a place in their prayers —and their purses also—to this admirable enterprise in the old birthplace of art and philosophy.

I have enjoyed every hour in Athens. Last Tuesday I climbed Mount Pentelicus, and from its summit looked right down on the famous battle-field of Marathon. It is as smooth as a race-course, and so small that Miltiades with his ten thousand Athenians could cover the whole front against ten times as many Persians. On my way back I rode through groves of classic olive and pine, and green vineyards. It seemed as if I might meet Sophocles going out to meditate a new tragedy, or Anacreon to compose a new song for the vine-dressers. The air was instinct with the memories and glories of the past. This little land of Attica once ruled the world with its genius. On the ruins of that wonderful commonwealth—after long dark centuries of ignorance and obscurity—a new Athens and a new Greece have sprung up. No land on the Continent of Europe has a stronger claim on our hearts, or excites a more thrilling hope for its future than the land in which Pericles builded, and Plato thought, and Phidias carved, and Paul proclaimed the Gospel of eternal life.

XV.

SUNRISE ON THE PARTHENON.

Athens, May 28.

AT four o'clock yesterday morning I aroused my fellow-lodger at the Hotel des Etrangèrs for a tramp up the Acropolis in time to catch the sunrise. The shadows were still lingering in the clefts of old Hymettus as we hurried across the open space between the Arch of Hadrian and the modest chapel of the American Mission. Rounding the hillside, we pass the ruined Theatre of Dionysius, with its forty carved marble seats—all empty. I would give something to know from which one of those tiers Socrates rose up to answer the gibes of the comedian. A little further on, we see the square-cut "Bema" from which Demosthenes once thundered. Let us be thankful that Lord Elgin could not kidnap that for the

British Museum. The smooth roadway leads around the south side of the Acropolis and close by the rocky spur of Mars' Hill. We see the actual steps in the rock by which Paul went up, and the spot where he must have stood when, within ten minutes, he delivered the sublimest speech that ever stirred the air of classic Greece.

We had to hammer pretty loudly on the gate to arouse the porter who keeps the entrance to the Propylea. Those walls once trembled to a louder alarm, when the explosion of a magazine sent the columns of that splendid structure flying in the air. Powder seldom wrought more mischief; for that ascending vestibule of richly sculptured Pentelic marble (which cost two millions of dollars and which was adorned with the statues of Phidias) was one of the marvels of Athenian magnificence. What a gorgeous spectacle it must have been when the Panathenaic procession swept up through that vestibule from the Sacred Way, with its trains of chariots and waving branches of the olive and the pine! Nearly a dozen of the Doric columns yet remain. Across the two central ones still hangs the solid lintel, twenty-two feet long and four feet in thickness. To have lifted that enormous block of marble to that position must have been no ordinary feat of engineering; but of far more interest to me than the columns is the pavement beneath them, worn smooth by the ceaseless tread of more than three and twenty centuries. Upon those identical slabs of white marble Pericles and Plato, Aristotle and Demosthenes have set their feet; the famous men of Rome—Cæsar, Pompey, Cicero, and Seneca—have trod there. Paul himself undoubtedly has walked there. The famous scholars of our times have gone in there. In fact, there is no other small spot on this round globe which has been pressed by the feet of so many of the mighty men of genius as the six square yards of that Portico of the Propylea.

We had no time to stop and moralize, for the sun was just beginning to peep over the northern end of Hymettus. A streak of his rays was touching the heights of Egina and Salamis. At the eastern brow of the Acropolis the late Queen Amalia built up a "Bellevue," or platform of stonework, from which a view can be got sheer down into the modern city, which lies upon that side of the sacred mount. We hasten to that "coigne of vantage" and look westward. The first rays of the sun are just kindling on the brown columns of the Parthenon. They are browned now by the hand of Time and the storms of over twenty centuries; but what they were when Pericles first set them there, in their flashing splendor, what imagination can conceive or pen describe? It will always remain an enigma that within a single century Grecian art and philosophy should have flowered out in the most consummate of their productions of genius and then straightway ceased to bloom again! All the greatest achievements of Athenian brains were wrought between the battles of Marathon and Cheronea, and that space does not cover more than the lives of a father and son, provided that they both lived seventy years. The only answer to this problem is that it seems to be God's plan to illuminate this world not by single stars, but by constellations.

After watching the golden sunlight for a few moments on the Parthenon, we walk on, amid heaps of broken columns and shattered friezes, to the northern brow of the Acropolis. A guard walks behind us, perhaps to see that we do not pocket a stray metope or triglyph; for since the Acropolis has been so plundered nobody is trusted there alone. A sly Britisher was detected, a while ago, in tossing rare bits of marble over the walls, which an accomplice was as slyly picking up down below. Let us be thankful, however, that neither Time nor Turk, nor Lord Elgin himself has ever succeeded in spoiling the exquisite northern colonnade and doorway of the Erectheum. Those columns are the perfection of the Ionic order. The carvings around that "Gate Beautiful" are the consummate masterpiece of delicate Greek art. No human hands ever excelled that workmanship. There is a mass of exquisite moulding and of delicate "egg-and-anchor" ornamentation, that looks more like lacework cut in ivory than any carving of ordinary marble. All the finest Ionic structures in the world for the last two thousand years have been only the copies of what those Greek wonder-workers wrought on that end of that little Erectheum within a single decade. They struck perfection at once, and all subsequent generations have done nothing but try to imitate their handiwork.

The rocky summit of the Acropolis is one mass of picturesque ruin. Of the forty-six superb columns of the Parthenon less than one-half are left standing. These are sadly marred; some of them snapped off in the middle. The broken fragments of the columns which were blown to pieces by the powder explosion caused by a Venetian bombshell, in 1687, lie scattered all over the hill-top. I climbed over piles of sculpture on which the workmen of Pericles had made their eyes ache; but mine ached still worse to see such marvellous productions dashed into destruction. Yet, after all the havoc that time and storm and shell and invading enemies have wrought, the Parthenon and the Erectheum still remain as incomparably the most magnificent ruins on the face of the earth. The sun that shone on them yesterday morning has never yet shone on their equal.

But, while we are on the Acropolis, let us take a glimpse of the Athens which stretches around us to the north and east. There is a bright day-dawning of promise in this beautiful city, with its broad, clean streets, elegant Parisian mansions, in imitation of Attic architecture, and with its showy Academy, and University, and public schools. There are seventy thousand people here now. When Parliament is in session, there will be many more. Down in that plain building on the corner of Sophocles and Aristides

Streets, the highest court of the city, still called the "Areopagus" will meet to-day. That large structure, surrounded by a fine park, is the Palace of King George the First.

While in cost, and adornment, it befits the modesty of a young kingdom, it contains some beautiful apartments. Upon its walls figures the fight at Navarino; and there are portraits of Capo D'Istria, and of Lord Byron who half redeemed the last months of his pitiable career by his devotion to the deliverance of Greece. Around the palace stretches a fine garden which is thrown open to the people every day.

Looking towards the Ilissus—which at this season is shrunk to a rivulet,—we see the fourteen surviving columns of the Temple of Jupiter. When the whole one hundred and twenty-four were standing---crowned with their Corinthian capitals—that structure must have been one of the most magnificent on the globe. Not far from these imposing ruins is the ancient Stadium, on whose race-course, the Olympic games were celebrated It is six hundred feet in length and one hundred in breadth; we can still see the terraced sides on whose marble seats, over forty thousand Athenians once sat, and cheered the victors in the games. Paul had such encounters in his eye when he exhorted the racers for an heavenly crown to "so run that they might obtain."

Let us turn to the opposite side of the Acropolis, and below us, near the road to the Pireus stands the Temple of Theseus —still in such perfect preservation that it scarcely shows the ravages of twenty centuries. As one looks at that exquisite Doric structure, with its columns and roof still complete, he can form some conception of what Athens must have been in the days of its matchless glory.

Of that ancient glory only a few other splendid fragments remain. The Parthenon is shattered. The Stadium is deserted. Plato's Academy is now a private gentleman's garden. The tomb of Socrates no man knoweth to this day. But as I descended from the Acropolis, and passed by the immovable rock of Mars' Hill on which the great Apostle once stood, I said to myself, —the glory of this world passeth away, but like that rock, the word of the Lord endureth forever!

XVI.

FROM ATHENS TO THE TYROL.

Salzburg, June 8.

THE last instalment of my twenty-one days of cruising over the blue waters of the Mediterranean was from Athens to Venice. We left Athens at five o'clock on the "Austrian Lloyd" steamer Minerva, and sailed out over the same waters which witnessed the defeat of Xerxes at Salamis. As the Acropolis and the Areopagus sank slowly out of sight, I felt that I was looking for the last time on the last spot trodden by Paul that I might ever see on earth. Early next morning we were off the rugged coasts of old Sparta; by noon we ran in close to the small town of Navarino, famous as the scene of the furious fight between the Greeks and the Turks in the war for Hellenistic independence. That whole voyage from Athens led over memorable scenes of conflict; for at seven in the evening we passed the bay in which Don John, of Austria, fought the battle of Lepanto, which was one of "the fifteen decisive battles of the world." By midnight we were at Arta—the ancient *Actium* where Augustus Cæsar routed Antony and Cleopatra and secured the imperial crown of Rome. Zante, with its picturesque little city and surrounding olive-gardens and currant-plantations, shone brightly in the evening sunlight. Then came Cephalonia, and the rocky isle of Ithaca which gave birth to Ulysses—and an euphonious name to the New York village which "Cornell" is making famous. Next morning we anchored close before the two castles in the harbor of Corfu. As I walked through the quaint old town, and inhaled the soft balmy atmosphere I did not wonder that Napoleon had pronounced the climate of Corfu to be the loveliest in the world. The steward of our steamer brought off several baskets of oranges freshly picked from the trees with the leaves sticking to the luscious fruit. He told me that the price was about one cent apiece; they were very fine, but I have found no oranges in the Mediterranean which equal those of Florida.

From Corfu, we had nearly two days of placid, dreamy voyaging over the smooth waters of the Adriatic; and my long cruise of two months from Marseilles ended in the harbor of Trieste. Like Marseilles, Trieste is a bustling, commercial city, full of bright cream-colored warehouses, stores, and mansions, with many grove-embowered villas on the surrounding heights. Trieste is the headquarters of the "Austrian Lloyd's" line of steamers; and after spending more than a fortnight on their decks I am happy to volunteer my testimony to their excellent management—with one shabby exception. On that Thursday night they packed a crowd of passengers into so absurdly small a steamer for Venice, that many from the first cabin were obliged to lie all night upon the deck. The churlish master of the boat could not understand English, and so he lost the benefit of many compliments that were paid him.

But if the accommodations of the cramped steamer were conducive to early rising, we had our compensation. At day-dawn what a view saluted my vision as I came on deck! All over the glassy Adriatic were floating the fishermen's boats with their red sails—such as we see in every Venetian picture—and before us in the morning light rose the domes and the Campanile of Venice. Gondolas swarmed about our steamer as we dropped anchor off the Doge's old palace, and in fifteen minutes we were paddling under the charming old Rialto. "After all," said an English fellow-traveller to me, "Venice is the most captivating city in the world." I demurred to this—for I had just come from Cairo and Jerusalem. The melancholy air of decay which lingers about the deserted palaces of what was once the splendid Queen of the Adriatic always saddens me in Venice. When the novelty of paddling in a gondola through the watery ways and close by the doorsteps of old musty mansions, is over, then the city becomes just a trifle monotonous. The first day is a delight and a marvel; the treasures of the Doge's palace and of ancient St. Mark are unsurpassed; after that ·Venice has no endless succession of picturesque scenes like Cairo, and no sublime memories to feed on like Jerusalem. The Italian Government are trying hard to revive Venice; but it is impossible to rebuild again the prosperity which once boasted of its fleets of merchantmen in every port.

At nine o'clock I was in the cars for Verona and Innsbruck. The vineyards, and gardens, and mulberry orchards, and grainfields were at the height of their June luxuriance. We sped on through Padua, and beautiful Vicenza, and Verona—over which the genius of Shakespeare still hangs like a morning star—and then we began to make our slow ascent of the foot-hills of the Tyrol. By six o'clock we reached the ancient city of Trent, the "Tridentum" of the Romans, and the town which the Papacy selected three centuries ago as the seat of its famous Ecumenical Council. It was a good stopping-place for the night, as I wished to see the grand scenery of the Brenner Pass by daylight. I found pleasant quarters at the "Hotel Trento," and sallied out, at twilight, to find the Church of Santa Maria. This venerable structure was the place in which the famous Council of Trent held its sessions from 1545 to 1559. I found it crowded with worshippers—over whom the candles at the grand altar threw but a dim light—and up in the chancel hung a large painting of the Council. A priest was reading prayers from a lofty throne or pulpit, and the people were responding with interludes of song. Their Italian and Tyrolese voices made such rich melody that I was glad that for once the organ held its peace. The next morning soon after six o'clock I was there again, and the church was filled as the evening before. Say what we will, these Roman Catholics put us Protestants to the blush in the matter of church-attendance. At that early service in St. Mary's Basilica were scores of day-laborers in their working-dress, mingled with the rich and the refined—all beginning the day together in a service of sacred devotion. Grant that there was no little of the sensuous and the superstitious in their service; still, it was the only way they knew to find God, or any comfort to their souls. Let us imitate their punctuality and their zeal before we hurl any more stones at their ignorance or their bondage to priestcraft.

After breakfast we quit our home-like hotel for the train; the courteous landlord accompanying his guests to the cars, purchasing tickets for the ladies, and then bidding us all "good-by" as if we were the guests of a private mansion. I wonder if it would do us Americans any harm if we should copy some of the pleasant amenities and courtesies that prevail in so many countries of Europe. A German hotel is really a school of politeness down to the waiters and the porter at the door. At the Hotel de l'Europe in

Innsbruck, every employé in the house rose and bade me "good morning" when I made my appearance, and a "good night" when I passed along to my room. Such little courtesies cost nothing, but they are very pleasant to a stranger in a foreign land.

My ride over the celebrated Pass of the Brenner was beyond all description. Ruskin's pen could not do justice to those deep emerald vales, those quaint chalets on the dizzy mountain-sides, and those mighty peaks above us clad with everlasting snow. We slowly wound up from one scene of enchantment to another until we had exhausted all our supply of superlatives and were content to gaze on the wonderful panorama in silence. On the southern side of the mountains the swift Adige shot and foamed along towards the Adriatic. After we had crossed the summit of the Brenner and begun our northern descent, another river kept us company with its rush and roar until we reached Innsbruck. That day's ride gave me the most complete sense of beauty that I have yet experienced during this tour. Switzerland is the land for sublimity; the Tyrol for a beauty that bewitches, but seldom overawes.

I spent three days at Innsbruck, which has two great attractions. One of them is the magnificent snow-crowned Alps that surround it. The loftiest of these—the "Waldraster"—is a massive pyramid of rock nine thousand feet toward the clouds. The other attraction is the monumental tomb of the Emperor Maximilian with its splendid sculptures and thirty bronze statues, which Thorwaldsen pronounced to be unequalled in Europe. It stands in the Franciscan church; and close by it are the grave and the statue of the heroic Hofer, the Tell of the Tyrol. His countrymen gathered around that monument last Sabbath, and gazed at it with veneration.

But alas for railroads and modern improvements! Hofer would not recognize his own kindred in their modern dress. Instead of the old, bright, picturesque Tyrolese costume which I once knew a few years ago, I now see only the prosaic imitations of their German neighbors. Only one genuine Tyrolese have I encountered during the last week who wore the red rig and graceful hat and feather of his ancestors. Yesterday I left Innsbruck by the new route, and had another enchanting day of mountains and verdant valleys; of fields purpled with flowers, and of swift streams foaming down the ravines. Late in the afternoon we began to see — far ahead — the lordly Castle of Salzburg on its lofty cliff — the only rival of Heidelberg for stateliness and grandeur. It stands like a giant sentinel overlooking a wide plain of surpassing loveliness. At its feet lies this romantic city, the birthplace of Mozart, and one of the most celebrated seats, in former days, of wealth and chivalry and song. Under the very shadow of that castle, I bid my readers "good night!"

XVII.

PRAGUE—DRESDEN.

Grand Union Hotel, Dresden, June 16.

FROM Salzburg I had rather a monotonous ride to Linz on the banks of the Danube. The noble old historic stream runs with a strong turbid current, and the scenery at many points on its banks is very fine. The next day brought me through Bohemia to Prague. It is Bohemia still, although under the Austrian crown; and the vast majority of the people still speak in the language of John Huss and Jerome. I found the city in its gala dress, with triumphal arches over the streets, and thousands of Austrian, Bohemian, and Belgian flags floating from the windows and house-tops. The Crown Prince Rudolph—the heir to the Austrian throne—had arrived on the previous day with the Princess Stephanie, his Belgian bride. As he purposes to make Prague his residence for some time, the Bohemians are in high feather at having a live specimen of royalty once more in the old palace of Maria Theresa. The next day he drove through the streets in regal style with his bride at his side, and amid the cheers of the populace. She is a pretty girl of seventeen, with a merry countenance, and promises to be exceedingly popular.

I was surprised to find Prague so large, so stately, and so modern withal; much of it is as bright as Brussels, and its shops are as showy as those of Paris. The town is built on elevated ground on both sides of the Moldau, and from the Palace walls—which stand on a lofty hill—it is really one of the most imposing cities in the whole Teutonic realm. To me it was chiefly interesting as the scene of the heroic career of John Huss. His presence still fills its atmosphere as the presence of Luther fills Wittenberg, and the august shade of Calvin still haunts the streets of Geneva. I hastened at once to the ancient "Teyne-church," where Huss often preached; it has been the scene of many a fierce conflict both of tongue and sword. Beside one of its venerable Gothic columns is the tomb of Tycho Brahe, the great Danish astronomer. His sextant is still preserved in the Jesuit College. I saw a fine specimen of his autograph in the Museum, and, what was of still higher interest, the original challenge of John Huss to his opponents which he affixed to the gates of the University. The Reformer wrote a strong square hand, and the precious document (which is only about six inches by four) looked almost like a leaf from a Hebrew Bible. Beside it lies a small manuscript of Ziska; and on an adjoining table is the first copy of the Scriptures ever printed in Bohemia. It is in clear type and bears on its title-page the date 1480. That was about midway between the martyrdom of Huss and the rise of Martin Luther. That Museum of Prague contains some fine picking for an antiquary. I looked with keen interest at some specimens of the iron flails used by the fierce followers of Ziska, and felt that it was enough for one day to have seen John Huss's challenge to the Pope and the Devil, and to have grasped the sword of Gustavus Adolphus.

Prague afforded me two days of unmixed delight in threading the streets of its ancient quarter, in crossing its crowded bridge from which Saint John of Nepomuk was flung, and across which armies fought for three centuries, and in climbing to the heights on which the great Wallenstein once lived in royal splendor. I found that quite too few Americans visit the grand old city of John Huss and Rudolph of Hapsburg; but it had a home-like look to me, to see in the reading-room of the pleasant Hotel d'Angleterre, a large English Bible and a file of the *New York Observer*.

The route from Prague to Dresden runs directly along the Elbe, and through the heart of that picturesque region known as the "Saxon Switzerland." An exquisitely beautiful region it is, with bold ramparts of rock, and deep green ravines, and romantic old castles on its steeps; but to call it after the same name with the region of Mont Blanc and the Matterhorn, is rather a hard strain upon language. It bears about the same resemblance to Switzerland that Trenton Falls do to Niagara. It takes a vast deal of beauty to reach the sublime. But that picturesque scenery along the Elbe I found to be an excellent preparation for the city of Dresden. I came here, not to discover historic sites or to be awed with majestic cathedrals, but to study art and to enjoy the finest single picture-gallery in Europe. Dresden simply means fine art; it is the Florence of Germany. Just as in Prague I hastened to the Church of John Huss, so on my arrival here I set off at once for "The Zwinger." On every previous trip to Europe I have been cheated out of Dresden; so I set my face speedily towards that huge pile of The Zwinger, which contains the splendid treasures which have been accumulating for a hundred and fifty years. The pecuniary value of the vast collection must be estimated by millions; outside of the Vatican no other roof covers so many of the masterpieces of genius.

I did not stop to sharpen my appetite with any "first courses" of inferior art, but struck at once for that room in the northwest corner of the edifice which contains Raphael's Sistine Madonna. Very few things in this world come up to our expectations. *That painting did;* I just put it in my memory gallery alongside of Rubens' "Descent from the Cross"; to my taste those are the two most perfect pieces of sacred art on this globe. Every one has a right to his own opinion, and every visitor to the Zwinger galleries has his favorites. After the peerless picture of Raphael, the six paintings which gave the most delight were Titian's "Tribute Money," Albert Durer's "Crucifixion," Rembrandt's "Manoah's Sacrifice," Corregio's "Holy Night," Battoni's

"Repentant Magdalen," and the "Ecce Homo" of Guido. As for the innumerable Venuses and Ledas, and other nude classicalities, they had better be turned over to my friend Anthony Comstock, or into the Elbe.

The same Titian who painted that wonderful head of our Lord in the "Tribute Money" had no business to smirch his pencil with those naked goddesses. Raphael kept his canvasses clean from such defilements. The gem of Albert Durer's genius is only about six inches square; but it is enough to give him immortality. The "Repentant Magdalen" of Battoni is copied in thousands of engravings in America; none of them give any idea of its exquisite charm of coloring. It is a face to dream about. Corregio's great feat is that he has made the face of the infant Saviour so radiant that it lights up the whole caravansera at Bethlehem. As for Rembrandt's painting of Manoah and his wife, kneeling with closed eyes and overawed by the angel's presence—it is one of the most solemn, devout and soul-moving pictures in the world. I shall always think of Manoah with a certain reverence, after seeing that wonderful portraiture.

Rembrandt was assuredly the greatest portrait-painter the world has ever seen. Next to him stands Vandyke. The masterpieces of these master-workmen are to be found here, and their works alone are enough to give celebrity to yonder galleries. I have been gazing this week at their productions, and at the marvellous productions of Raphael, and Titian, and Guido, and Durer, and Rubens, just as I gazed at the Parthenon at Athens, and said to myself, "What has become of the creative genius that did these things? Why can the age that invents telegraphs and bridges oceans with steamships, do nothing but *copy* the art of centuries gone by?" In one short century little Greece taught the world how to build and how to carve marble; in another brief period the great painters taught the world what painting is; their skill died with them and they have left no successors. Our age has other work to do: "To everything there is a time," and the time for rearing Parthenons and painting Madonnas has gone by, never to return.

Dresden is rich in historical relics as well as in works of art. I spent some hours yesterday in the Johannean Museum, looking at the magnificent suits of armor worn by the old Electors of Saxony, and the trappings of their horses resplendent with gold and jewels. The Elector Christian II.'s armor was of solid silver. Under one glass case were the swords of Peter the Great, Charles XII. of Sweden, and Macaulay's hero William, Prince of Orange. In another case were Martin Luther's sword and drinking-cup. The grand old fellow had no business with either. There was a remarkable collection of shoes in one room; among them the dainty slippers worn by Empress Maria Theresa, and the coarser footgear worn by the philosopher Kant. Napoleon's boots worn at the battle of Dresden were there, and also his coronation slippers made of satin and richly embroidered with gold. Judging from these, the foot that trod down Europe for fifteen years must have been very small.

After examining the rich collection, I went down into the "Green Vault" under the Palace to see the gorgeous display of gold and silver ornaments and rare jewelries. There are enough rubies, pearls, diamonds, and showy trinkets there to make the belles of Fifth Avenue and Saratoga crazy. If Solomon could have seen Dresden, he might have added another chapter on "The peculiar treasures of kings," and their "vanity and vexation of spirit." To-day I leave this fascinating city for Wittenberg, the home and burial-place of Martin Luther, where he used a stronger weapon than a sword to make war upon principalities and powers, and spiritual wickedness in high places.

XVIII.

THE LAND OF LUTHER.

Wittenberg, June 18.

DURING neither of my previous visits to Germany have I been able to see the region especially associated with the greatest events of Luther's career; so I shaped my present tour that it might include both Prague and Wittenberg. The look at the home of Huss, the pioneer of the Reformation, was a good prelude to the home of the Great Reformer.

Wittenberg is a quiet city of twelve thousand inhabitants, on the banks of the Elbe, about midway between Dresden and Magdeburg. But few Americans visit it, for I had to look back some distance on the register of this "Hotel of the Golden Vineyard" before I could find a Yankee name. Dresden is Parisian, but Wittenberg is thoroughly

German. The railroad keeps a respectful distance from the gates of the town, as if it would not disturb the dreamy quietude of the old cradle of the Reformation. As the one-horse omnibus jogged slowly toward the ancient Elsterthor, the driver swung his whip toward an oak-tree, surrounded by a grass-plat and a few flowers. That tree marks the spot where Brother Martin burned the Pope's fire-decree, on the tenth of December, 1520. The blaze of that burning "bull" was pretty distinctly visible from the Vatican.

The little inn at which I was set down stands on the market-place. In front of my window are two statues, about a hundred feet apart. One of them, erected fifteen years ago, represents a slender figure, robed in a gown, with a countenance almost emaciated and wearing a saintly expression. Upon the pedestal is inscribed, from the Epistles to the Ephesians: "Endeavoring to keep the unity of the Spirit in the bond of peace." On the other side is written: "I will speak of Thy testimonies also before kings, and will not be ashamed." That slender, seraphic figure is Philip Melancthon, who was the gentle and beloved *Jonathan* to the burly psalmist and warrior who stands on the twin pedestal, a few yards off. A genuine Teuton is that robust character, planted firmly in his bronze shoes and holding his finger to the open page of God's Word. The short, taurine neck and heavy jaw mark the holy obstinacy of the man. The inscriptions on the pedestal are exceedingly happy. Underneath the open Bible is inscribed (as if Luther himself were just speaking it from his bronze lips): "Believe the Gospel." That is the very message which German theology and philosophy need most to hear and to heed to-day. The east side of the monument bears Luther's famous words: "If this be God's work, it will endure: if it be man's it will perish." On the west side is carved the immortal motto: "*Ein feste Burg ist unser Gott.*"

The partnership of these two great leaders of the Reformation, which is marked by the similarity of their monuments, holds good all through the town. Walking up the "College-strasse," I came upon a three-story house, old within and modernized without. "Here lived Philip Melancthon" is written on the front. Into that narrow hallway the jolly face of Luther must have been thrust many a time, when some new idea was to be discussed with Brother Philip or when some racy scandal about Tetzel or Eck had come to Brother Martin's ears. With many a boisterous laugh that house has rung, I'll warrant. There was infinite fun underneath Luther's well-lined ribs. There must have been almost hourly intercourse between the two men, for just a few steps beyond Melancthon's house I came to an arched entrance to an open court. In that court a teacher was watching the gymnastics of a few boys. Before me was a large building, called the "Augusteum" and now used as a seminary for ministers. The middle rooms on the second floor are a part of Luther's original dwelling. He lived there while professor in the University, in 1508, and his good friend, the Elector Frederick, presented the house to him. A generous soul was Frederick, for I saw at Dresden a superb cabinet, ornamented with carved work and jewels, and also a gilded drinking-cup, which he gave to his beloved friend the Reformer.

In the doorway of the Augusteum sat an old lady, knitting, with a pretty daughter at her side. The young *fraulein* took a key from a nail and led me up a stairway, through an ante-room; and then unlocking an ancient door, showed me into a large room, with low ceilings. In one corner stood an enormous iron stove, eight feet high, covered with historical groups in bas-relief. In the other corner stood a large oaken table. These are the only surviving pieces of furniture in the apartment which was once filled with the presence of the mightiest man of the sixteenth century When on the cold winter nights that big table was wheeled up beside the big stove.

and the big head was bent over it in study, then God's Word was unloosed into the Teutonic tongue. Sometimes the Bible stands open to the Epistle to the Galatians, and then he takes a turn at the "Commentary." Brother Melancthon has his reserved seat by the stove, and sometimes, when Brother Martin breaks out into a snatch of "*ein feste Burg*," it almost drowns the howling of the blasts without. Good wife Catherina brings in some hot potations occasionally, I suspect: for there is a drinking goblet still preserved in the room and I saw another one in the Museum at Dresden. One of the most unique relics in Luther's room is the autograph of Peter the Great, in chalk, on the door-frame. There was enough of the Norseman about Luther to suit Peter's ideal of the "konning-man."

After I had enjoyed the quaint old room and possessed myself of the photograph of Cranach's portrait of the Reformer, which hangs in an adjoining apartment, the *fraulein* took me down the street to the ancient

MARTIN LUTHER.
(From the original Portrait in his house at Wittenberg.)

Schloss-kirche. It stands close against the infantry barracks. Upon the original doors of this church Luther nailed up the famous ninety-five theses, in 1520; but during a bombardment of Wittenberg by the Austrians the doors were burned. King Frederick William replaced them with metal doors, bearing the original Latin text of the theses. Within that church Luther's ashes slumber, beneath the central pavement. Close by him sleeps Brother Melancthon. The partnership was never broken. Loving in their lives, in death they are not divided.

Last evening, at sunset, I went down again to the ancient church. A few of the simple German town's-folk (just such folk as Luther used to preach to here) were strolling past, out to a public garden in the suburbs. I seemed to see the burly Reformer, as he came to that spot, three hundred and sixty years ago, with the immortal theses in one hand and his hammer in the other. He does not dream himself what results are to come from that simple deed. With sturdy strokes he sends home the nails, until the ring of that hammer begins to startle Germany out of the slumbers of the Dark Ages. Germany has never gone back into that nightmare of superstition; but Protestantism on the Elbe and the Oder is *not* broad awake to-day. That hammer needs to ring again.

This morning, early, I walked around to the old Stadt-kirche, in which Luther often preached, close to the market-place. A service was going on and but few were present. I contrasted sadly the small gathering with a crowded service at the same hour (a fortnight ago) in the Romish Church at Trent. The Catholics attend church at least fivefold more than the Protestants on the Continent; but the service in the Stadt-kirche interested me deeply, because the " plain song " was the same that Luther and his neighbors used to sing there. In fact, the neighbors themselves were close beside me, for many of Luther's intimate friends and brother professors lie buried under the church or close to its walls. All round the outer wall of the building stand their moss-grown tablets, with epitaphs barely legible. Some of these worthies of the sixteenth century are represented in queer effigies of stone, either clad in armor or in scholastic robes. Here a head is broken off; there, an arm. Time has dealt roughly with these stout old protestors; but to me, this morning, they seem to be living still and their spirits still haunt the ancient church in which they once crowded to hear Brother Martin denounce the "Man of Sin." Nay, Luther himself seems to abide here still. All Wittenberg is full of his spiritual presence, and, as I look out of my window this bright June morning, I can imagine him as walking with lumbering gait down yonder College-strasse, with a roll of his MS. German Bible under his arm. He walks across the market-place, stops to salute Brother Philip with a "*guten Tag*," and then vanishes out of sight.

XIX.

HAMBURG TO COPENHAGEN.

Copenhagen, June 23.

I FOUND Wittenberg not only interesting from its great historic past, but from its representative character as a quiet industrious town occupied by the middle class of the German people. As there are infantry-barracks in the town, I saw rather more than the average number of soldiers in the streets, but they are quite too abundant everywhere in Kaiser William's dominions. This swarm of locusts, in martial toggery, is devouring the substance of the Empire. We in America have our full share of dram-shops and demagogues, but let us thank God that we have not the additional curse of a vast standing army. At sunset I strolled out of Wittenberg to ornamental gardens in the suburbs, where the town-folk were regaling themselves with promenading in the public walks, and some of them with tall tumblers of beer. The Germans are a domestic, cheerful, and festive people, and delight in assembling together in such beautiful parks and gardens as every town can boast. I really pity them when they come to America; they must sadly miss such a public "platz" as I saw in Innspruck, Wittenberg, and on a grand scale in Hamburg. Their attempts to reproduce these places of social resort in our country are but sorry attempts at the best; but even though they fail I am not surprised that they make the effort. It is a part of a German's very life to enjoy his social hour in a park or a "Volk's Garten," and even though those Wittenbergers imbibed more beer than we teetotalers fancy, yet I saw no drunkenness or boisterous carousals.

My next stage was to Hamburg by rail. I find the German railways admirably managed, and moderate in fare. There are very few "first-class" cars; the second-class are really luxurious, and the first-class are left to the princes and the fools. Except in those carriages that are marked "Nicht-rauchen" (no smoking) or "for ladies," there is perpetual fumigation with pipes or cigars. Smoking has become almost universal in the Orient and over the continent of Europe. In Turkey, Egypt, and Syria the ladies are greatly addicted to cigarettes; there is not one man in a hundred who does not indulge in his narguilèh if he can afford it. Mohammed prohibited wine, but I suspect that pipes will be a prominent feature in an Oriental's Paradise.

Hamburg is a great bustling and showy city, with nearly half a million of inhabitants, including the suburbs. It is the chief commercial city on the continent, and becoming immensely rich. Around the "Alster Basin" are sumptuous hotels and private mansions; the parks are filled with fine equipages; and five thousand merchants and shippers crowd the Exchange every day from one to three o'clock. The finest building in the city is the St. Nicholas (Protestant) Church, a florid Gothic structure, with a spire four hundred and seventy-three feet high. There are only two loftier spires in Europe—Cologne Cathedral and St. Ouên at Rouen. I attended service there last Sabbath morning, and although the noble building has seats for two thousand and standing-room for as many more, there were not two hundred persons present! I went around afterwards to "St. Peter's," an elegant church, in which at least fifteen hundred were in attendance. After the sermon—delivered under a rich ancient canopy—the congregational singing in German plain-song was very grand. The architectural display of Hamburg—especially in the way of elegant private residences—has surpassed my expectations. In the finest portion of the city is the "Alster Basin," a small lake, surrounded by the principal hotels and promenades. This Basin extends for about two miles, growing narrower until it becomes no wider than the East River at Astoria. It is lined with beautiful villas and gardens, and a sail past these delightful grounds is the most attractive recreation I found there. Every ten minutes a sort of omnibus-steamer started from in front of our hotel for "Ravenstrasse," or "Bellevue," or "Eppendorf," or other of these suburban resorts. Merchants or bankers, after business hours, go on board these little steamers with their wives and children, and for a few dimes enjoy a sail that is as pleasant as an excursion to Staten Island. No commercial craft enter this miniature lake, which is used exclusively for pleasure-travel.

Although street-cars (or "tram-ways," as they call them in Europe) originated in America, yet we may learn something from the way in which they are managed in Hamburg. A line starts from in front of the Exchange every five minutes, and carries you through the beautiful narrow park (which almost surrounds the city) towards Altona. The finest horses I saw in Hamburg were driven before some of these cars. In the rear of each car is a sort of lobby for cigar-smokers; and no one is allowed to enter the car unless there is a *seat* for him or her. The road has a single track for part of the way, and when one car meets another, it turns out on the Belgian pavement, and is easily thrown back again on the iron rails by means of a small guiding wheel in front of the car. In one of these luxuriously cushioned cars I never paid more than three cents fare; and if we could have anything approaching to this in comfort, we Brooklyn folk would not be so intensely anxious to see an elevated railway. Hamburg would not endure an hour what Brooklyn has patiently submitted to for twenty years.

Like all the other German towns, Hamburg has its monument to its soldiers who fell during the Franco-German war of 1870. It is the most touching in conception of any I have ever seen on either side of the ocean. A bronze figure representing "Germania" is holding a laurel over a dying grenadier who is just falling in the saddle of a horse that also lies dead upon the field. The figures of both horse and rider are superb. Just behind them is a dying infantry-soldier, and beside him an artillery-man has fallen with his rammer in his hands. It is altogether a pathetic poem wrought into bronze. The work was executed by Schilling of Dresden, and as a stroke of genius, is equal to the famous equestrian statue of Frederick the Great in Berlin.

Hamburg ranks next to London, Liverpool, and Glasgow, in the extent of its commerce. Over six thousand vessels enter its capacious harbor every year. The chief articles in which its merchants deal are sugar, coffee, iron, grain, butter, hides and fancy goods. From its wharves about thirty thousand emigrants set sail for America during every twelvemonth, and a majority of these are Germans. Some leave the Fatherland to escape service in the army; others to avoid heavy taxation; others in order to become land-owners (and not tenants) in our great West; and others still from preference for a republican government. They are, in the main, a thrifty, honest and industrious addition to our American population. But they carry over with them their lax ideas of the Sabbath and their inbred religious formalism; too many of them are enough tainted with "scientism" to become utter skeptics. They cannot be reached by our ordinary agencies, and unless they are approached by German preachers and missionaries who can address them in their own language, they will simply become fresh recruits to our growing army of Sabbath-breakers, and rejectors of gospel-truth. To meet that stream of emigration which pours towards us from the Teutonic empire, the American churches should be establishing German theological schools, and training the right men for the work.

From Hamburg I came last evening to this capital of the Danes by way of Keil. Bishop Peck of America, who is on a visit to his Methodist brethren in the north of Europe, was my fellow-passenger. We reached Copenhagen at ten this morning and within an hour I was in the Thorwaldsen Museum. The name of this peerless sculptor of modern times is to Copenhagen what the name of Luther is to Wittenberg. Of none of her sons is Denmark so proud; and well she may be, for Thorwaldsen is the one sculptor of our era who, if he had lived in Athens, would have been selected by Pericles to carve the frieze upon the Parthenon. Up in these cold northern latitudes bloomed out that wonderful genius whose productions adorn the walls of unnumbered homes in every clime.

XX.

THE CITY OF THORWALDSEN.

Copenhagen, June 24.

THIS city might well be called *Thorwaldsen*, for it is filled with his presence as Wiemar is with the presence of Goethe and Potsdam with that of Frederick the Great. Not an hour passes in which his name is not heard; not an art-store in town that is not filled with the photographs of his matchless works; and thousands, like myself, come hither mainly to feast their eyes on the marbles which his hand has carved.

Copenhagen is a larger city than one would expect to find as the capital of so small a country as Denmark, for it contains 235,000 inhabitants. Its streets are bustling with business, for these Danes are an active, commercial people, exporting no small amount of grain, tallow, cattle, horses, and very mischievous cherry-brandy. The architecture of Copenhagen is not imposing; not one really grand edifice adorns the squares; its palaces wear a shabby look; and a monotonous uniformity pervades the whole town. How two such beautiful women as the Czarina of Russia and her sister, the Princess of Wales, should have issued from yonder dingy-looking palace is a conundrum. But it is still more remarkable that this prosaic old seaport of the Norsemen should have produced the greatest sculptor of modern times, Bertel Thorwaldsen! We might say the greatest *known* sculptor of any age, for Canova, Dannecker and Chantrey were not to be compared with him, and we don't know *who* produced most of the masterpieces in marble which have come down to us from ancient times. Thorwaldsen claimed that his ancestors were kings of Iceland, but his own father was a ship-carpenter; and the boy Bertel early learned to handle the tools with which his father carved figure-heads for Danish merchantmen. He went early to Rome, and for years pursued his studies of art in utter obscurity. By and by he executed that grand statue of "Jason and his Fleece," which I saw to-day, and then he awoke to find himself immediately famous. Thenceforward his chisel was busy for almost forty years; and his native Denmark, proud of his genius, gave a home in one of her palaces to the greatest man she has ever produced.

Yesterday, as soon as I had arrived in Copenhagen, I hastened off to the Museum which was erected expressly to contain the productions of his chisel. It is a gloomy looking edifice on the exterior, and the interior is severely plain. In the hollow square of the quadrangle is the great sculptor's tomb. Four granite slabs enclose a little bed of earth, planted with ivy, and on one of the slabs is the simple name BERTEL THORWALDSEN. The whole building with its treasures is his real monument. On entering the building you see in the vestibule the long Triumphal Entry of Alexander into Babylon, a series of bas-reliefs, executed by order of Napoleon, and worthy of a place on any of the friezes of ancient Athens.

Soon after I went into the smaller cabinets that contain his masterpieces, I began to come upon those exquisite originals whose photographs are hung in thousands of American parlors and libraries. In one cabinet was his famous "Night," with the two cherubs asleep on her shoulder and the owl poised in the air behind her drooping wing. On the opposite wall is "Morning," with the cherub bearing the torch to light up the dawn. A little farther on I came to the bas-reliefs representing "Spring," "Summer," "Autumn," and old "Winter" warming his benumbed fingers over the brazier of coals. Then, a few steps farther on, I encountered the "Ganymede and the Eagle," the "Hebe," and the "Shepherd Boy," and the "Three Graces." All these had long been as familiar to my eye as the City Hall of Brooklyn, or the spire of my own church. Yet the originals are so vastly superior to any photo-

THE CITY OF THORWALDSEN. 223

graphic copies, that they burst upon me as entirely new revelations of beauty! They were not marble; they seemed like flesh and blood that had turned white. The dog that stands beside the shepherd boy looks as if he could breathe, and you almost expect to hear him bark! The little cupids that are playing their roguish pranks in a "Love-nest" are as individual in the expression of their sweet faces as any half-dozen babies brought into an infant school on anniversary day. It is not art; it seems actual *life*.

But the sublimest of Thorwaldsen's productions are not contained in this museum. They are in the "Frau Kirk," a Protestant house of worship often attended by the royal family. The building itself is in the Greek style, and is very attractive. On the front of the pulpit is inscribed, in golden letters: "Blessed are they that hear the Word of God, and keep it." That motto ought to be written on every pulpit in America; it would furnish a hint to us ministers as to what we should preach, as well as to our congregations to carry home the truth and practice it.

On the platform at the end of the church is an exquisite kneeling Angel, that holds in her hand an escalop-shell of marble—used as a baptismal font. It is a dream of beauty. Behind this figure, in an alcove, rises the somewhat colossal figure of the *Risen Christ*. Above his majestic head is the inscription, "This is my Beloved Son, hear ye him." That glorious form—the only statue of our divine Lord I have ever seen that is worthy of its subject—is immediately before the congregation every Sabbath when they assemble for worship. Along the sides of the nave—about a dozen feet apart—are ranged Thorwaldsen's celebrated "Twelve Apostles." The figure of Paul is commonly accounted the finest; but that of Thomas (who stands with his finger pressed on his lip in an attitude of *doubt*), seemed to me superior to all the others. John has too womanly a beauty for a "son of thunder." Because he was the "beloved disciple" there is no reason to imagine him as either effeminate or seraphic. No one of the group has any more resemblance to any other than would any twelve living men who should meet in a Council or a Presbytery. Thorwaldsen never repeated himself. He had a wonderful instinct in catching the varied expressions of the human countenance, and his five hundred or more different statues are each entirely different from the other. He seemed equally at home, too, in classic and in sacred themes for his chisel. Once he selected himself for his subject, and the noble figure of Thorwaldsen—chisel in hand—by his own consummate skill will always remain as the great artist's best likeness. He must have been a man of commanding nobility of face and presence.

I have devoted the whole of this letter to this extraordinary genius, for several reasons. One is that he is more to every visitor in Copenhagen than all the rest of the city combined. Again; I am sure that hundreds of my readers who have copies of his works in their houses will be gratified to know more about the original masterpieces. But above all, I desire to pay my humble tribute to an artist who never prostituted his transcendent genius to an impure or demoralizing purpose. Much of the highest art at Florence, Venice and Dresden is lascivious. Over the walls are sprawled whole shoals of nude goddesses and nymphs and other unclean beasts. But Thorwaldsen portrayed a Love that never degenerated into lust. His chisel was never wanton. His magnificent galleries can be traversed by any father with his daughter at his side. He never profaned even the ineffable Lord of glory when he attempted to portray him in marble; and whether the man were a Christian or not, he consecrated his chisel to a higher and holier purpose than any sculptor in modern times. I am thankful that during a journey that has included Jerusalem and Athens and Wittenberg, I have also seen the peculiar treasures of the *City of Thorwaldsen.*

XXI.

NORWAY.

Christiania, June 27.

WHEN my congregation sent me abroad, it was their desire that I should not only see as much of the lands of the Bible as the lateness of the season would permit, but should also extend my tour to the north of Europe. I had also been anxious to get at least a good glimpse of Scandinavia. To a Norwegian there is no land so beautiful as his own Norway. He is ready to maintain that no waters are as picturesque as the fiords that indent the western coast of his native country and that the mountains which overhang them are a fair match for Switzerland. Few Americans ever venture into the home of the Norseman, but those who have done so always bring back glowing accounts of the grandeur of the scenery, and of the cordial hospitalities of the people.

Norway ought to command a deep interest in our country, for no nationality in Europe is sending so large a proportion of its people to settle in America. The Norwegians are a prodigiously energetic race, who feeling straitened by the sterility of much of their soil, and the severity of their climate, are swarming over to the generous prairies of our boundless west. Their own country is eleven hundred miles long, but a large portion of it is bleak and barren; only the southern half is capable of rewarding the industry of the agriculturist. The Scandinavian emigrants bring to us not only the habits of frugality and thrift but an intense loyalty to the Protestant faith. As far back as the tenth century King Hako the Good introduced Christianity into Norway after his temporary residence in Britain. He endeavored to overthrow the worship of Odin and Thor, and his successor Olaf the Holy went so far as to pull down the temples of those old Norse divinities. Since the Reformation of the sixteenth century, Norway has been so intensely Lutheran that until lately, no places of worship belonging to any other sect or creed were allowed to exist. Religious liberty is now guaranteed to all; but nineteen twentieths of the people still subscribe to the doctrines of the Augsburg Confession.

Until my arrival here I had always supposed that Norway had quite lost its national existence, and became absorbed as a part of Sweden. But this is not the case. Norway maintains its autonomy entire. It has a Storthing or parliament of its own which enacts all the laws of the realm. It has its own army and navy and post-office departments. The postage-stamps issued by the government of Sweden are no more current here than they would be in New York. In this city of Christiania—which is the capital of Norway—there is a palace to which King Oscar comes during a part of every year, to administer the government over his subjects on this side of the border. A Norwegian flag—somewhat similar to the Swedish—floats over yonder palace, and from the fortifications in the harbor. The union of Norway to Sweden is simply an union by treaty under which the two nations agree to be governed by the same sovereign; his official title is "King of Norway and Sweden." The similarity of race and religion between the two nationalities has brought them into such a close alliance that for all practical purposes they are as really one as the people of Scotland and of England.

After I had satiated myself with the fine sculptures of Thorwaldsen in Copenhagen, I set off for this beautiful city. A swift steamer starts for Christiania every Friday morning, and I found the "Christiania" a model boat with a model captain. As we came out of the city we passed a British fleet (with the Duke of Edinburgh on board) which was anchored on the precise spot where Lord Nelson fought the battle of Copenhagen in April, 1801. Campbell, in his magnificent lyric on the battle, describes the slaughtered sailors who "sleep full many a fathom deep, by the wild and stormy steep of Elsinore." But Elsinore is twenty miles from the scene of the engagement, and has about as much of a "wild steep" as the wharves of Jersey City. Campbell had no genius for geography, for in his "Gertrude of Wyoming" he describes palm-trees on the banks of the Susquehanna!

As we passed Elsinore, which lies at the narrowest part of the "Cattegat," we ran in close to the old castle of Kronberg, on whose platform or water-battery Hamlet saw the ghost of his murdered father. To-day there is no Danish prince promenading on that battery, and no British sailor sleeping in the waves beneath. After we had passed the narrows of the Cattegat we came at once into that strip of water called the "Skager Rack," which separates Denmark from Norway and Sweden, and which used to be the scene of the nautical exploits of the old

Norsemen. Over those waters Harold Harfrager sailed with his fierce Scandinavians to the conquest of England two centuries before William the Norman was born. Along all those rocky shores the beacons of the Vikings once blazed. These Scandinavians have always been a race of water-dogs sporting among their fiords and boisterous bays like the seals on the rocks of Alaska. Norway is to Europe very much what Maine is to our American Union, both as to northern situation, picturesque island-studded coast, and the hardy, adventurous character of its people.

On Friday afternoon our steamer ran its sharp bow in among a shoal of rocky islets, and after threading its way for several miles, we came suddenly into the harbor of Gothenburg. It is a thrifty commercial city, built most picturesquely on the rocks, with a few strips of emerald vales and wooded parks lying in between. Lumber was piled on the the wharves, and mackerel fishermen were moored alongside, just as at Portland or on the Kennebec. Gothenburg is one of the starting-points of Wilson's line of steamers for England, and thence for America; one of the firm tells me that they ship annually forty thousand Scandinavian emigrants to our country. I would gladly exchange ten Catholic Corkonians for one of these sturdy industrious Protestants. If they could only be cured of some loose ideas in reference to the Sabbath—which they hold in common with all the Lutherans in Europe—and of their liking for strong drink, they would be the very best element in our immigration. On our steamer a decanter of free whiskey was placed on the table alongside of the decanter of water, and most of the ladies as well as gentlemen took a wine-glass of "old rye" before they tasted either food or wines. While in the Mediterranean, I found wine to be the universal beverage, except in the seaport towns, where there is a villainous consumption of Holland gin and New England rum. In Germany the use of wines and beer is enormous. Here at the North, whiskey and other powerful alcoholics are the popular drinks. There is an isothermal line in national beverages as in climate. The Saxons and Scandinavians and Sclaves are the races most addicted to alcohol.

On Saturday morning we awoke among the charming scenery of the Fiord that leads up from the sea to Christiania. The banks of the fiord were a combination of pine-clad mountain and verdant valley, with a sprinkling of bright Norwegian villages. Christiania lies superbly on the hills at the head of the fiord, the old Castle of Agershaus standing out as a figure-head in front of the town. As soon as we landed I went around to another wharf to see an American friend off on the steamer for the North Cape, the Polar Sea, and the midnight sun. But why go a twenty days' journey to Hammerfest, when there is almost a midnight sun here at Christiania? In this northern latitude (which is higher than Labrador), at this season of the year, the night has folded its sable wings and flown away. Last evening I was able to write with ease by an open window at eleven o'clock! Even at midnight it was not dark, and the city authorities did not light the street-lamps. A person with good strong eyes could easily read a newspaper through the whole twenty-four hours in the open air. But in midwinter the daylight does not last over six or seven hours.

At this Grand Hotel I have been greatly gratified to meet my Brooklyn neighbor, Prof. E. P. Thwing, who is on a tour of exploration among the churches and Young Men's Christian Associations and benevolent institutions of Scandinavia. I was getting a little tired of listening even to polite Germans in dislocated English, and hailed the society of a brother Yankee with genuine satisfaction. Prof. Thwing tells me that he saw snow six inches deep at Drontheim last week! The air has a keen edge still, even in the sunshine. I do not wonder that this austere climate sends thousands to America.

We rambled up to the Palace, which stands at the head of the Avenue in front of our hotel. In this palace the King Oscar II. resides when he visits the Norwegian half of his double kingdom. In front of the Palace stands a fine equestrian statue of Charles John XIV., better known as Marshal Bernadotte. On the pedestal is the inscription, "The love of my people is my reward." Out of all the brood of sovereigns on whose heads Napoleon placed an uneasy crown, Bernadotte was the only one who was able to retain it; and his family occupy the throne of Sweden and Norway to-day. It is a suggestive fact that while Napoleon squandered a million of lives in order to conquer territory for France, she does not now hold a single acre of it all! She has even lost Alsace and Lorraine by the sword. In the meanwhile the Puritan's Bible and plough have gained possession of a vast continent.

We found in the palace the same stereotyped series of throne-rooms and ball-rooms and gaudy upholsteries that all "kings' houses" have to display. But from the palace-roof we had one of the most enchanting prospects that I have seen since I left Salzburg. Before us was the city with its hill and vale; beyond was the harbor bestudded with islands, and to the right lay "Oscar's-hall," a Summer château of the King, surrounded with the brightest green that nature ever dyes. On a high ground to the left is the City Cemetery, laid out much like our own. I visited it on Saturday towards evening, and found hundreds of ladies there with watering-pots, freshening the flowers and grass in the plots for the Sabbath. This is a beautiful Saturday evening custom in Christiania.

Yesterday the burial-grounds needed no artificial irrigation, for it rained bountifully. We attended an English service in the chapel of the University, an institution which enrols a thousand students. There were forty persons at the service; the ritualities were exceedingly long, the singing exceedingly thin, and the discourse very much like the music. On our way home we saw five hundred people gathered in the park under umbrellas, and listening to a military band. Handbills posted about the streets and headed "Norske Travel-klub," announced an equestrian performance for the Sabbath afternoon, and the theatre was open in the evening. Here, as elsewhere on the Continent, the morning of the Sabbath is thought sufficient for all purposes of worship by the majority of Protestants, and the latter half of the day is devoted to socialities and amusements. In this regard some Romanists take a higher stand than their Protestant neighbors; for in Innspruck I saw the Romish churches crowded at five and six o'clock in the Sabbath afternoon. What the Protestantism of Holland, Germany and the North wants is a fresh quickening. In Sweden I am told there are tokens of a new evangelical life; if so, I shall be glad to record it in my next. Oh, for another Luther! And when the next Luther comes, Heaven grant that he may come without any gilded "drinking-horn," and with the true idea of a Sabbath!

XXII.

STOCKHOLM.

Grand Hotel, Stockholm, July 5.

OUR twenty-four hours' journey from Christiania, by rail, was very tedious, but as we drew near to Stockholm, the tasteful villas in the suburbs gave token of the beauty of the city before us. I do not wonder that the Swedes are proud of their "Venice of the North." When the old Norseman, Birger Jarl, founded it six hundred years ago, he had the good taste to select a site that would meet alike the demands of beauty, of commerce, and of military defence. One end of the city encompasses beautiful Lake Mælar; another part, including the Palace, is on the central island; still another on the mainland to the north; two other islands have their share of the aquatic town; and all these various waters are alive with boats and spanned with bridges. The city abounds in parks, and the parks abound in statues, fountains, and flower-beds. In order to protect his new capital, Birger Jarl drove down piles or "*stocks*" among the "*holms*" or islands; hence the name Stockholm.

I have had a most happy week here. Immediately opposite this Grand Hotel (which is one of the finest in Europe) is the Royal Palace. It is reached by the Noorbro bridge which spans one of the many waters of Stockholm and which is known as the North River. I spent an hour in wandering through the royal apartments, one of which, called the "White Sea," is a magnificent saloon, a hundred and eighteen feet long, entirely in white and gold; when illuminated with lights and gorgeous costumes it must be a fairy scene. I was most interested in examining the private room of King Bernadotte, filled with his various knicknacks and just in the condition that the old warrior left it. On his bed lies the blue military

Stockholm. From Mose-Back.

cloak that he wore in all his campaigns, and slept under every night for thirty years. It covered him when he fell into the slumber of death. It is ordered that the old cloak shall never be taken from the room, but the moths are carrying it off piece-meal. The present King Oscar II is an honest, capable ruler, who spares no pains to make himself popular with the people. The Queen is a devout Christian, and the King's sister, Princess Eugenie, is a leader in various religious and philanthropic movements. There is not a purer Court in Europe.

Over on the Riddarholm Island stands the venerable church which is called the Westminster Abbey of Sweden. It is a plain brick structure with a lofty spire of open iron-work. This is the sepulchre of the kings and the mighty men. In a sarcophagus of green Italian marble lies the dust of that glorious hero of the Protestant faith, Gustavus Adolphus, and over it are an hundred banners won on bloody fields. The rash and brilliant Charles XII. lies on the opposite side of the nave; but Gustavus Adolphus is the popular idol. His manly figure appears, in either bronze or marble, in public squares all over the kingdom. At the National Museum they show you a little brown nag that he rode in his last fatal fight at Lutzen; and close by the stuffed remains of the horse, lie the hero's clothes stained with his blood His name will be linked in history with William the Silent, Washington, and Lincoln.

I had heard much of the great evangelical quickening which has been going on in Sweden during the last dozen years, and I am sorely disappointed in not meeting Pastor G. E. Beskow, who is one of its leading spirits. He belongs to the National Lutheran Church and is known as the Spurgeon of Sweden. His spacious church, which is usually crowded with over three thousand auditors, stands in the rear of this hotel; but the building is closed for repairs, and the eloquent pastor is absent from the city. The failure to meet this eminent leader of evangelicalism has been compensated by the delightful intercourse I have had with Professor Kanute Broady of the Baptist Theological School and many of his brethren. Broady is better known here by the title of "Colonel," as he commanded a regiment in the Army of the Potomac during our civil war. A finer specimen of a manly, genial Christian gentleman I have never met than Col. Broady. Last week the Baptists—who number about twenty thousand communicants in Sweden—held their annual convention here. They kindly sent for me, and gave me such a greeting as these warm-hearted Norsemen only can. Col. Broady was good enough to say in his speech of introduction that my religious articles had been circulated in the Swedish language for the last twenty years. This was chiefly grateful to me as another vindication of the policy of taking some time every week from pastoral duties for the religious press. A type is often equal to ten thousand tongues in spreading Gospel truth.

Later in the same day I attended the annual collation of about one hundred Baptist ministers at the Berzelius Hotel. It stands on a charming little Park which contains a statue of Berzelius, the famous Swedish chemist. After my address at the dinner, a special prayer was offered for America by the venerable Mr. Palmquist, who is the founder of Sunday-schools in Sweden; it was a most fervent, soul-stirring petition. The next day these same brethren invited Dr. S. F. Smith of Boston, Prof. Thwing and myself, to join them in an excursion to Upsala. This ancient University town lies forty miles north of Stockholm; near it are the huge mounds which are the traditional tombs of Odin, Thor, and Freya—who are embalmed in our English calendar in the names of Wednesday, Thursday, and Friday.

It is vacation-time at the University; so I did not see the Professors or any of the fourteen hundred students. But I did see the Botanical Garden, and the tomb (in the Cathedral) of *Linnæus*. The trees and shrubs he planted are blooming still. Close by the Botanic Garden stands his marble statue; his benign face has a singular sweetness, as if he had studied flowers so long that their beauty was reflected in his countenance. There is a marked advance in the theological teachings of the University towards the evangelical interpretation of God's Word; and Rationalism is growing weaker, both there and among the ministers of the National Church. As I had to return to Stockholm at an earlier hour than our party, I had for companion in the cars a devout Swedish pastor, whose stock of English consisted of a few Bible texts. He commenced the conversation by saying, "Blessed are the poor in spirit, for theirs is the kingdom of heaven." To this I assented; and then he presently added—"Goodness and mercy do follow me all the days of my life, and I shall dwell in the house of the Lord forever." It was a brief conversation, but I have heard railroad talks much less edifying than his.

Last Sabbath morning I attended St. Jacob's Lutheran Church which stands near the statue of Charles XII. It was well filled, and I observed some of the Dalecarlian peasant-girls there in their picturesque costume. At least six psalms were sung during the service, and before each singing, two little boys climbed up a ladder and hung the number of the psalm on the pillars each side of the pulpit. The sermon was to me in an unknown tongue, but the pastor was fervent in manner, and all the people attentive to hear him. In the evening I preached to an overflowing crowd in the Baptist Church; Col. Broady acting as my interpreter. It was my first experience in that kind of preaching by one sentence at a time, and then pausing for its translation. I felt like a bird tied to a gate-post, that is jerked back every time it should get to the length of its string. But the genial countenances of the Scandinavians before me were an inspiration; and when they sang "Come thou fount of every blessing" in Swedish and to our familiar tune, I felt a little moist about the eyelids. I have formed a deep affection for these simple-hearted Baptists, who are enduring hardness for Christ's sake. Most of their pastors receive very small salaries and only preach at all by sufferance. The ecclesiastical laws of Sweden do not recognize or protect them; and if a priest of the Established (Lutheran) Church chooses to complain of them, they are liable to arrest and imprisonment! I saw two of these godly men who had been "in bonds" and fed on bread and water for the crime of preaching without permission. Happily this bigoted spirit of persecution is dying out.

Yesterday I celebrated my Fourth of July by dining with our hospitable American Minister the Hon. John L. Stevens. It was a sad day to us, for we had just received the terrible tidings of the attempted assassination of our noble President. The news awakens a profound sensation in the city, for Sweden is warmly allied to America. If such be the feeling here, what must it be in my own beloved land! God grant that long ere this reaches my readers, the life of the foremost man in our Union may be out of danger!

In April, 1865, the news of Abraham Lincoln's assassination was telegraphed to our foreign Ministers—among others to the late Hon. William B. Kinney, Minister to Italy. He happened to be in the same town where the late Czar Alexander of Russia was stopping. He hastened to the Czar's apartments, and said, "Sire! President Lincoln is assassinated!" The Czar leaped from his chair, and exclaimed "Good God! that cannot be so." When Mr. Kinney showed him the telegram, he broke out into a fervid eulogy of Lincoln and wept like a child. How little he dreamed that the same diabolical blow was yet to strike down himself!

This afternoon I leave this delightful city for Gothenburg by the Gotha Canal, which traverses the finest scenery in Sweden. My travelling-companion is to be Dr. S. F. Smith, the author of "My country, 'tis of thee." The venerable man is returning from a visit to his son, a missionary in Burmah.

XXIII.

THE WARM HEARTS OF SWEDEN.

Gothenburg, July 8.

MY last letter did not by any means exhaust the noticeable attractions of Stockholm—a city that grew upon me every hour. One afternoon I went over to the "Mose-backe" an elevated public garden on the island of "Sodermalm." This is a favorite resort of the citizens and affords one of the finest outlooks of the Venice of the North. On my way thither I passed the Hornsgatan, in which (at No. 43) the celebrated mystic Emmanuel Swedenborg long resided. The house has been removed, but the summer-house in the garden,—which was the philosopher's favorite place of study—still remains. There he saw visions and dreamed dreams for many years; it is a sort of Mecca for all members of the "New Jerusalem Church" from various quarters of the globe. But although Swedenborg was a native of Stockholm and spent most of his life there, he left but a handful of followers. His mysticism was too impalpable for the solid and devout sense of the Swedes; and they were too well anchored in the knowledge of God's Word to be led away by his philosophical vagaries.

The hero of the popular worship in Sweden is a man of the very opposite stamp—Gustavus Adolphus. In the very centre of the city, mounted on his bronze war-horse, stands the great Protestant leader, and on the anniversary of the battle of Lutzen (in which he fell) thousands of Swedes gather around this statue and sing the noble war-ode which he taught his soldiers. The old hero's ashes sleep in the Riddarholm church, and bear this happy inscription, "*In angustiis intravit, pietatem amavit, hostes prostravit, regnum dilatavit, succos exaltavit, oppressos liberavit, moriens triumphavit.*" "He braved dangers

—loved piety—overthrew his enemies—enlarged his kingdom—exalted his nation—liberated the oppressed, and triumphed in death." To him it is chiefly owing that Sweden and Norway are to-day the most intensely Protestant nations on the continent.

From the Mose-backe heights one gets a fine view of the new National Museum, which fronts the water on the Blaiseholmen terrace. It is built of granite and marble at a cost of over half a million of dollars. The vestibule, which is flanked by colossal statues of Odin, Thor, and Freya, is one of the most imposing that I have seen in Europe. In a long series of apartments are exhibited the various relics of the aborigines of Sweden. In one room are displayed the relics of the bronze age (three centuries before the Christian era); of the earlier iron age, A.D. 600; and of the later iron age, from the sixth century to the tenth. Other rooms contain an extensive collection of ecclesiastical robes, censers, chandeliers, and various religious vessels in copper, silver, and gold. The history of Sweden may be studied—as in a grand system of object-teaching—in the halls of that magnificent edifice. The collection of antiquities has been largely increased by a law which compels every finder of a valuable relic or curiosity to deposit it in this Museum—its full value always being paid in cash. In the Picture-gallery, I was vastly more interested by the works of Lindegren and the other artists who depict Swedish life, than by all the importations of old Italian masters. I had been surfeited with "Holy Families" long before.

Another building in which all the Stockholmers take a just pride is the new Royal Library on the Humlegarden Park. Among the curiosities there is the "Codex Aureus," a Latin manuscript of the Gospels in gilt Gothic characters, and dating back to the sixth century. There is also a copy of the Bible which is claimed to be the hugest manuscript volume in the world. It is written on three hundred asses' hides, and cost the labor of the monks in a Bohemian monastery for four centuries. This monster volume is over two feet in thickness and it would tax a Constantinople porter to carry it. There is a copy of the Vulgate with abundant annotations in the handwriting of Martin Luther; and in that Library I saw, for the first time, one of the original books printed by Faust himself. It is a well printed copy of Cicero de Officiis and bears the date, 1461.

Much as I was charmed with the scenery of Stockholm and its historical relics I was still more charmed with its people. Those of my countrymen who met Fredrika Bremer and Jenny Lind during their visits to America, saw in them the type of character which gives such attractiveness to Swedish society.

I have come into contact with the warm Christian hearts of this people during the last ten days in a way that I shall gratefully remember to my dying hour. I had heard of the evangelical awakening in Sweden during the last dozen years, but I was not prepared to find so fervid an atmosphere up in these regions bordering on the frozen poles. During the week I have seen much of such men as Professor Canute Broady, Prof. Theodore Truve, Pastor Lindblom, and Mr. Palmquist, the founder of Swedish Sunday-schools. On Sabbath evening last when I preached to a thronged audience in the principal Baptist church, it reminded me of a fervid revival service in America. "The people want to hear about nothing but Jesus," said Broady to me before I began, and I tried not to disappoint them. As the English sovereign is current coin in every land, so the name that is above every name is the key to every Christian heart around the globe.

On Monday came the terrible tidings of the attempt upon the life of our noble President. It produced a deep excitement over all Sweden, for there is a peculiarly cordial fellowship with a country to which forty thousand Scandinavians emigrate every year. During this week it has been very easy to recognize the telegrams from Washington in the Swedish daily papers—for they are printed in bolder and more conspicuous type than any other intelligence. The report of that fiendish pistol has literally been heard around the world; from Christian America too, in a time of peace, it has an awful reverberation. What a volume of prayer is ascending heavenward that a life so precious may be spared!

My companion in Stockholm has been the venerable Dr. S. F. Smith of Boston, the author of our national hymn, "My country, 'tis of thee." He tells me, by the way, that he wrote the lines now so famous while he was a student at Andover, and at the request of Lowell Mason—who asked him to compose something that would go to the air of "God save the King." Who changed the name of the air to "America," I do not know. As Dr. Smith and myself were to leave for Gothenburg on the same steamer—by the Gotha Canal—the noble-hearted brethren offered us the kind compliment of a farewell entertainment. As we had prayed and sung together, it was arranged that we should break bread together; and a fine collation was spread at the "King Charles Hotel." Many of the active pastors of Stockholm, Christian laymen and their wives were present, and farewell addresses were spoken that made our hearts like water. Not content with this demonstration at the Hotel, our irrepressible friends must needs accompany us to the Riddarholm wharf to see us off. The little steamer was packed with passengers, each of whom was blessed with friends. So the wharf was black with the people and white with waving handkerchiefs. I really felt as if I had known those loving friends for twenty years instead of ten days; and up in this far-away land such a demonstration of kindness in the Master's name was like an added verse to the Epistles of John the Beloved.

Steaming away from our friends on the quay, we had a two hours' sail through beautiful Lake Mælar; it is lined with the villas of the wealthy residents of Stockholm, as the Hudson is lined with those of the millionaires of New York. After leaving the Lake our steamer threaded its way, during the night, among the rocky islets in the Baltic. At "Mem" the real canal commences; it is about fifty feet wide and ten feet deep, and it ascends and descends seventy-four locks between Stockholm and Gothenburg. After a few miles of canal we entered Lake Roxen, a charming sheet of water, in which we sailed for an hour. At the end of the Lake we reach a series of locks, ascending like a stairway for nearly one hundred feet. The passengers all quit the boat for an hour's run on shore, while the locking process goes on. A charming tramp we have too, over fragrant clovers whose blossoms mingle with daisies and a dozen varieties of flowers that load the air with perfume. Some of us wander off for half a mile to visit the ancient Wreta church, in which three old Norse Kings that died seven centuries ago lie buried. On our return to the boat, a Swedish peasant girl brings us refreshing tumblers of milk from a tidy farm-house. The peasantry are a hard-toiling, frugal set, who earn a small return from their cold soil, but they are a virtuous, church-going people, and in solid worth are not surpassed by the peasantry of any land.

The whole afternoon of Wednesday was spent in alternate lake and canal until we reached the thrifty iron-manufacturing town of Motala. There we enter Lake Wetter, and after a halt beside the old Castle of Wadstena—built by Gustavus Vasa in 1545—we cross the lake in half an hour to Carlsborg. As we approach Carlsborg at ten o'clock, the sun has just set, but it has left an *afterglow* that fills the sky with brightness, and dyes the placid waters of the lake with a crimson glory. The light does not vanish away, even at midnight, but lingers on until it meets the day-dawn. The moon—almost full—instead of rising up toward the zenith as she does with us, turned backward and set below the horizon at eleven o'clock. These singular celestial phenomena arise from the fact that we are so near to the Arctic circle and to the region of perpetual day.

Yesterday morning found us sailing across Lake Wenner, which is almost an hundred miles long. We had a fifty miles' experience of the lake and then entered the canal again at Wennersburg. We were now approaching the famous falls of Trolhattan, which are fairly equal to our Trenton Falls, in wild and picturesque beauty. While the boat is descending the locks, we all sally off to see the magnificent series of rapids and cascades, which extend for a quarter of a mile. The highest of the falls is about forty-four feet, but the volume of the water is so large, and the rocks throw such superb jets into the air that the effect is like a section of the Rapids of Niagara. Trolhattan signifies the "home of the water witches," and surely they could not have found a more bewitching abode. During the last four hours of our trip, our little steamer was descending the Gotha River. I had heard much in America of the fascinating scenery on the Gotha Canal, and I acknowledge that it equalled my highest expectations. It is a succession of pictures for two and a half days that fill the photograph gallery of memory for a lifetime. The Americans who consume all their time in Paris and on the Rhine make a sad mistake that they do not set their faces toward such a city as Stockholm, such scenery as the banks of the "Gotha," and such a people as these noble-hearted Scandinavians.

This morning found us at the wharf of Gothenburg—the Liverpool of Sweden. It is a busy city, and in its central square stands the figure of its illustrious founder, Gustavus Adolphus. This is the chief point of departure for the forty thousand emigrants who annually embark for America. My good steamship, the "Romeo," lies yonder—with steam up—for Hull and dear old England. Several hundreds of emigrants are thronging her forward decks; the wharf is crowded with kinsfolk to bid them farewell; on their boxes I see such names as "Michigan" and "Minnesota." I do not wonder that many of them are weeping; for after a fortnight's sojourn in this land, I can hardly keep back the tears at leaving the *warm hearts of Sweden.*

XXIV.

THE GREENTH OF ENGLAND.

"The Ivy House," London, July 14.

AT Gothenburg I took the fine new steamship "Romeo," of Wilson's Line, for Hull in England. We had a smooth passage of forty-five hours, and the most luxurious state-rooms I have found during my journeyings. Having passed forty-two nights in the berths of steamers since I left New York—often "shelved" on a narrow board that suggested the processes of an undertaker—I am happy to pay this grateful tribute to the sleep-inspiring comforts of the Romeo. We ran up the Humber, which looks like pea-soup, against a strong tide, and I felt a buoyant thrill when my feet stood again on English soil.

Hull was interesting to me as the birth-

THE GREENTH OF ENGLAND. 263

place of William Wilberforce, and as the town in which my beloved friend Rev. Newman Hall (during his early ministry) wrote his world-known " Come to Jesus." It was first suggested to him by hearing a group of primitive Methodists singing, at a meeting in the open street, the simple revival ditty of "Come to Jesus just now." To write that blessed little guide to inquiring souls was glory enough for one lifetime. I easily found the ancient smoky mansion in which the noble Wilberforce first saw the light; for it is now used for law offices, and is called the " Wilberforce Building." There is also a lofty monument to the Emancipator in the heart of the city.

I have had many a charming ride through the greenth of old England in the summer; but never one that equalled my ride this week on the Midland road through Yorkshire, Derbyshire, Leicester, Rutland, Northampton and Bedfordshire up to London. The day was perfect; the summer sun absolutely glorified the verdant fields, and hedgerows, and lawns, and groves of oak; the beauty of the scenery almost blinded me! As we passed through the sweet emerald valley of the Ouse, the air was perfumed with the memories of Cowper and Newton and Legh Richmond. Then we ran into Bedford where Bunyan dreamed the wondrous dream. That day was one unbroken festival of eye and soul; and after all I had seen in the Orient, and the Tyrol, and the Northern lands, I said to myself—"The paradise of rural beauty is to be found in Shakespeare's and Milton's England."

A great many elements enter into the composition of an English landscape. In the first place the Creator gave our British ancestors a goodly heritage of mingled hills and vales and running streams that are blended together after the most perfect ideal. Then he bestowed a climate so mild and yet so moist that the foliage and the grass are kept up to the color of a deep emerald during the largest portion of the year. Such midsummer droughts as we suffer are very rare in this climate. For five centuries cultivation has been busy upon these charming fields,—planting hedges, and trimming them, grouping trees for picturesque effect, building walls, turning waste places into gardens, and so beautifying every acre that as Emerson says, "England is finished with a pencil instead of a plough." An universal taste for flowers prevails; in the humblest cottage-windows are boxes of scarlet geraniums; over almost every doorway climb flowering plants, and as for the rural railway-stations they are an horticultural show. Every station-master would seem to be a florist. It made me ashamed of the forlorn shabbiness that surrounds most of the railway depots in my own land.

Nature has done wonders for the English landscapes, and art has wrought in harmony. Here an old Gothic church lifts its tower amid the oaks; there an Elizabethan mansion heads an ascending lawn; there a graceful bridge of stone arches some clear silvery Avon or Dee or Trent; even if a cottage be two centuries old it wears its thatched crown gracefully. To this perfection of rural loveliness our mother country has arrived after twenty generations have expended their utmost toil, and taste and skill.

One shadow is beginning to spread over this sunny picture. The "landed interest" of Great Britain is becoming involved in pecuniary difficulties and embarrassments that threaten ruin to many landlords, and have already driven some into bankruptcy. For many years land increased in value until it was regarded as the most profitable and secure of investments. But the immense importation of breadstuffs and beef and bacon from American prairies has so diminished the profits of British agriculture that the farmer and the land-owner are alike the sufferers. Rents are coming down. Farming lands have lost thirty and often forty pér cent of their value. Added to this has been an almost uniform succession of bad harvests. Many of the great estates are embarrassed with mortgages and other liens upon the land; and under these accumulated difficulties ancient families of the "gentry" are forced to sell off the manor-houses in which their ancestors have dwelt for many generations. To-day the most urgent and exciting questions, not only in Ireland but in England too, are those which concern the ownership and the pecuniary management of all those beautiful green acres on which my eyes feasted with such delight.

As I passed through the very heart of England on my way from Hull, I could not but think how rich had been the mental and spiritual harvests gathered from those old historic fields! Nearly every town has placed books in our libraries, or in some way enriched our memories. When I read the name of "Kettering" on the station-sign I thought of old Andrew Fuller's eight volumes of solid theology. Northampton suggested Doddridge and his "Rise and Progress." At Bedford I was in the birthplace of both John Howard and the "Pilgrim" of John Bunyan. Not far away were the green fields where Cowper mused over the "Task" and the "Olney Hymns." Robert Hall, Lord Macaulay, Marvell, and Kirke White had all been born and reared in the regions through which we ran; and from amid the smoke of Sheffield had come forth the musical notes of Elliott and Montgomery. All these memories added new charms to the verdant landscape that smiled under the summer sun.

I was glad to reach London in time for the annual gathering of the friends of Temperance at the Sydenham Crystal Palace. On Wednesday about fifty thousand members of the various organizations—Templars, Bands of Hope, the League and the "Alliance," with numberless badges and banners —swarmed in the Palace and the surrounding Park. Sir Wilfrid Lawson, the champion of the Local Option movement in Parliament, presided at the meeting in the great music-hall and made a capital speech. He is a man of ready wit and indomitable perseverance. I feel quite sure that somewhere in an English quarry is the stone which shall yet build to Sir Wilfrid a monument as well deserved as that of Wilberforce at Hull. After his speech I was called on to say a few words for America and the only thing I shall note here was the tremendous cheering that followed my mention of the name of President Garfield. The whole audience rose, and fairly shook the building with the roar. You can hardly conceive in America what a profound and universal feeling has been aroused throughout Great Britain by that fiendish assault on the life of our President. It renews and repeats the days in 1865, when Lincoln fell under the assassin's pistol. From the throne to the cottage one deep, heartfelt sympathy and righteous indignation has been awakened.

Returning to town with Sir Wilfrid I found him greatly encouraged by the progress of temperance sentiment in Britain. Especially is the movement spreading among the churches and the more influential classes. For several days I hope to enjoy the pure air and outlook of this Hampstead Hill on which my brother Newman Hall's "Ivy House" is situated. He resides five miles from his church (on Westminster Road) in order to obtain wholesome air and quiet. From my window I can see colossal London spreading away for twelve miles toward the south! The roar of its life—with four and a half millions of souls—is like the roar of Niagara.

XXV.

DRIVES ABOUT LONDON.

Hampstead Hill, July 18.

ALTHOUGH I have visited London several times during the last thirty years, I never before had such an adequate conception of its enormous magnitude. It is really a dozen cities rolled into one. The residents of "Hoxton" know as little of those who live in the district of "Clapham," several miles away, as the people of Brooklyn do of the dwellers in Newark, New Jersey. I am staying up here on cool, breezy Hampstead Hill—so near to the country that we can look out over green fields to Harrow. Turning southward, we look toward St. Paul's lofty dome, and in that direction, for many miles we see the smoking chimneys of the mighty metropolis.

It grows at the rate of 100,000 inhabitants each year!

This part of the city is rich in historical memories. Once Hampstead and Highgate were clear out of town. I passed yesterday a gin-palace that stands on the site of the house to which poor Steele (one of the authors of the "Spectator") used to flee out of London to hide from his creditors. Mr. Hall drove me the other evening through Highgate, which was a rural suburb forty years ago. We passed the former residences of Lord Erskine, the king of British lawyers, and of Lord Mansfield, the king of British judges. A little farther on we passed the modest brick house in which Coleridge dreamed away the closing years of his life. Thither came Charles Lamb and Carlyle to hear the old poet-philosopher harangue by the hour. Five minutes walk brings you to a two-story mansion called Landerdale House; there lived the notorious Nell Gwynn, and thither came that royal rake Charles II. to pay her clandestine visits.

Exactly opposite this dwelling of a king's mistress, stands "Cromwell House," which the great Protector built for his son-in-law, Ireton. The stairway is very broad, and rich in carved woods; up it the iron heel of the greatest ruler England ever had, has tramped many a time. A few rods from Landerdale House are three stone steps left beside the pavement; they are all that is left of the residence of Andrew Marvell, the grand old poet of Puritanism. They lead also to that "Garden" about which he penned this exquisite poem.

"What wondrous life is this I lead!
Ripe apples drop about my head;
The luscious clusters of the vine
Upon my mouth do crush their wine;
The nectarine and curious peach
Into my hands themselves do reach:
Stumbling on melons as I pass,
Ensnared with flowers, I fall on grass.

Here at this fountain's sliding foot,
Or at the fruit tree's mossy root,
Casting the body's vest aside,
My soul into the boughs does glide.

> There like a bird it sits and sings,
> And whets and claps its silver wings;
> And, till prepared for longer flight,
> Waves in its plumes the various light.
>
> "How well the skilful gard'ner drew
> Of flowers and herbs this dial true!
> Where, from above, the milder sun
> Does through a fragrant zodiac run;
> And, as it works, the industrious bee
> Computes his time as well as we.
> How could such sweet and wholesome hours
> Be reckoned but with herbs and flowers!"

I set my foot on those three steps with reverence, for the feet of Oliver Cromwell and of John Milton had often trod there. But what a combination of names in one spot—Cromwell and Charles Stuart—Milton and Nell Gwynn!

On our homeward way we passed an inn called the "Spaniard," and attached to it is a small building looking like a porter's lodge. That was a favorite spot with Dr. Johnson when he used to come out of busy London to the rural regions of Hampstead Hill; since his day that diminutive room has echoed to the merriment of Charles Lamb, Charles Dickens, and many another literary celebrity. As we came opposite an old mansion half-hidden among the trees, Mr. Hall pointed to a projecting bay-window in the second story and said, "When the Earl of Chatham was suffering from a severe mental depression he was brought to that house, and for weeks he sat in that bay-window looking out upon these trees." And so every rood of our drive brought us in contact with some spot associated with the most illustrious names in English history and letters.

On Thursday we drove down to Hyde Park at the hour when all the rank and fashion there do congregate. We found the great drive was being kept clear by policemen, and it was lined by an expectant crowd. Presently her Majesty Queen Victoria appeared, in her royal coach and four, and attended by the splendid retinue of Life-Guards. The Queen has become very stout, and the fair brown hair is turning gray. The royalest thing about her is her pure, kind, exemplary womanhood. She was on her way to a garden-party at the Prince of Wales's Marlborough House, and we drove down there to see some of the "high-bloods" arrive and depart. Among them was the celebrated beauty, Lady Dudley; she is certainly very fair and comely, but I could easily find her match in Brooklyn.

From thence we went to the Metropolitan Tabernacle to hear Mr. Spurgeon deliver his Thursday Evening lecture. It was a hot week-day evening in midsummer, and yet over two thousand people were present! Mr. Spurgeon is now in vigorous health, and gave us a capital extemporaneous talk upon Ezekiel xlvii. 11. During his lecture he told a racy anecdote about a quack inventor of a cough-medicine, and he mimicked the fellow's cough so well that it created some merriment. But the discourse was exceedingly pungent, and close to the conscience. After service I had a pleasant chat with him, and hope to spend part of Saturday with him at his house near Sydenham Palace.

Our next drive was to Parliament. There was a tolerably full House, and the Irish Land bill was under discussion in Committee of the whole. John Bright spoke briefly; the ruddy cheeks of the great Commoner bespeak good health, and his hair is as white as snow. During a brief talk with him in the lobby I ventured to say to him that the greatest mistake of his life was his refusal of the invitation of our Government to visit America after our civil war. Much of the debate was conducted by the Irish members —the irrepressible Parnell speaking very often. Mr. Gladstone came in late, attired in a full suit of gray, and looking very happy as he greeted his ministerial colleagues. But the tedious pettifogging of the Irish members presently aroused him, and he rose and let fly a most indignant rebuke. The greatest of living statesmen is full of fire, and is good for another ten years of public service.

On Saturday we went to Putney—near which the University boat-race is always run —to attend the opening of a new wing of the "Royal Hospital for Incurables." The country around Putney is charming, and the Hospital stands in a velvet park, such as verdant England only can boast. The lions on the occasion were Prince Arthur and his royal wife; they are known as Duke and Duchess of Connaught. The band of the Coldstream Guards gave us capital music, and the audience were addressed by the Prince in a very fluent and excellent speech. His young wife—who was dressed with excessive and becoming plainness—sat by a table and received the donations which were handed to her by the guests, as they filed along. Over $20,000 was handed in! The Prince presided at the luncheon in a large tent, and gave us another good speech. He looks exceedingly like his royal mother.

Yesterday was a bright, golden Sabbath. As my dear friend, Mr. Hall, had given up his week to me, it was but fair that I should preach for him. "Christ Church, Westminster," is a noble edifice and its tall Lincoln Tower is conspicuous over all of southern

London. In the audience yesterday I recognized that eminent Christian philanthropist, the Hon. Samuel Morley, Member of Parliament. Mr. Morley will visit our country in August, and is sure of a hearty reception. He stood by us manfully during our war. Adjoining Rev. Newman Hall's church is "Hawkestone Hall," which he uses for his prayer-meetings and Sunday-school. They have also several mission-schools. The singing yesterday was admirable — being conducted by a choir of forty persons, and in the hymns the congregation joined. Brother Hall—although a Congregationalist—continues to use the liturgy which his predecessor, Rowland Hill, introduced. He is the one clergyman in England who *always* prays for our President and for the "people of the United States of America." With what deep feeling did the large assembly join in the prayer for our beloved Garfield yesterday!

Between the services at Christ Church I went over to Westminster Abbey, where, at 3 o'clock, the Bishop of Kentucky delivered a very eloquent discourse. After the service the chorister lifted the mat on the central aisle of the Abbey that I might see the tomb of the heroic missionary to Africa, *David Livingstone*. I had a few words with Canon Farrar, whom I hope to hear next Sabbath. He is a tall, muscular man, with genial face and ringing voice. Calling to leave our cards at the Deanery, we were saddened to learn that Dean Stanley was worse, and grave apprehensions are felt in regard to his situation. The death of Dean Stanley would be a calamity not only to Britain, but to all Christendom. I loved him more than ever when I looked yesterday at the tablet to John and Charles Wesley, which he had erected in Westminster Abbey.

It contains the medallion portraits of the twain founders of Methodism. Beneath a bas-relief—representing John Wesley as preaching to a crowd of Cornish miners—is the inscription "the whole world is my parish." At the foot of the tablet are his last words—"Best of all, God is with us."

XXVI.

CAMBRIDGE—THE SAVOY—MR. SPURGEON.

London, July 25.

ON Wednesday I took a delightful run to Cambridge. My first point was to visit Christ Church College, at the farther end of whose velvet grounds stands the mulberry-tree which Milton planted. They have heaped a mound around the veteran's trunk and propped up his limbs, but the leaves show no signs of withering. Thence I went to feast my eyes once more on the exquisite tracery in the stone roof of King's College Chapel—the gem of Gothic art. But oh! what a vision of loveliness is the park of Trinity College, with its emerald turf, and lofty oaks, and winding river Cam! Under those shades strolled Henry Martyn and his friend Charles Simeon; among the graduates of this famous college were Lord Bacon, Sir Isaac Newton, Byron and Macaulay. The chapel had just been locked up, but one of the servants admitted me by a back-door, and I found myself in an apartment where Bacon, Whewell and Macaulay in solid marble, were seated side by side. Bacon sat with uplifted head as if meditating the "Novum Organum"; Prof. Whewell was seemingly busy over a mathematical problem, and Lord Macaulay was thrusting his fingers into a volume whose marble leaves were a happy emblem of the immortality of his own History of England. I peeped into the great dining-hall, whose walls are lined with the portraits of illustrious graduates; across the passageway came savory odors from the huge kitchens. In the University library is the "Codex Beza"; on its wall hangs the sweet boyish face of Henry Martyn; I found William Pitt's room up in "Pembroke," but I was sorry that I could not find the room in which young Oliver Cromwell put on his armor for a conflict with tyranny which gave and received "no quarter."

London overflows with history at every turn. Every time I walk down the hill to the Underground Railway Station I pass a seat on which poor Keats often sat, and a row of trees under which he loved to walk in melancholy reverie. The other day I turned out of Fleet Street into Bolt Court, to find the house of Dr. Samuel Johnson. A well-dressed youth of seventeen said to me gravely, "Up at the head of the Court in Gough Square is the house in which Dr. Johnson used to live, but I don't know just *where he lives now.*" The poor fellow looked a little sheepish when he read the inscription on the front of an old brick house—"Dr. Johnson once lived here; he died A. D. 1784."

The Thames embankment is now the finest drive and promenade in the city. Upon one side of it, in a most unfavorable position, stands the Egyptian obelisk—the twin of ours in Central Park. I walked along the embankment, among the trees and flowers, until I came to the statue of Robert Raikes —which was erected last year, by the friends of Sunday-Schools. The benefactor of the little ones will soon find himself in good company, for it is proposed to place quite near him, a statue of John Wycliff, the morning star of the Reformation. As I turned off the embankment towards the Strand, I discovered, on my left, a small burial-ground, and just beside it a quaint stone church with a stumpy tower. Inquiring of a passer-by what it was, he informed me that it was the old church of "The Savoy." Happy indeed I was to find that the march of improvement which is sweeping away so many landmarks, had spared this choice bit of antiquity. Away back in the reign of King Henry the Third, the famous Savoy Palace stood on that spot. Edward the Black Prince brought the King of France there as a captive in 1356; John of Gaunt lived there; and during his residence the poet Chaucer was married there to a lady in the household of the Duchess of Lancaster. Stow tells us that no house "in the realm could be compared to it in beauty and stateliness." Wat Tyler's rebels burnt the palace, but Henry VII. rebuilt it as a hospital. After the restoration of Charles II. the celebrated Savoy Conference was held in that building, for the revision of the Liturgy. Episcopalians and Nonconformists joined in the work, and Richard Baxter drew up, in a few days, that reformed Liturgy which Dr. Johnson pronounced one of the finest compositions of the kind he had ever seen.

Of all these five centuries of history the little church of "St. Mary le Savoy" is the successor and survivor. Thomas Fuller, one of the wittiest and most original of British authors held the weekly lectureship of the Savoy in the days of Charles First and has added the fragrance of his genius to the savory memories which cling around the quaint old structure. Few places in London carry one farther back into the shadows of the past than this. The turmoil and traffic of the Strand were roaring within a few yards of me; but in that quiet side-nook I seemed to be still in company with the chivalrous Black Prince, with Master Chaucer and his bride, and with the godly men who gathered around Richard Baxter to shape the petitions of the English Church. Perhaps two or three centuries hence some tourist from Japan may explore Trinity Church in New York with the same interest that I visited the ancient "Savoy."

Before I dismiss these historical explorations let me say that I paid a visit to Abney Park Cemetery the burial place of famous Nonconformists. Dr. Thomas Binney slumbers there, and Dr. Raleigh, and Sir Charles Reed, and John Vine Hall, the author of the "Sinner's Friend." It was once the private park of the Sir Thomas Abney whom Dr. Watts went to visit, and the visit was protracted to twenty or thirty years. In one corner of the park is a mound of earth sheltered by a spreading tree; a granite tablet bears this inscription "This was a favorite retirement of Dr. Isaac Watts."

There the pensive bachelor loved to read and meditate, and there he composed some of his immortal hymns.

I cannot get accustomed yet to the loss of "Temple Bar," and that frightful object, like a witch of Endor which has taken its place, is no improvement. But a change for the better is the removal of the Young Men's Christian Association from their old and cramped quarters in Aldersgate Street to the spacious Exeter Hall in the Strand. The original rooms are indeed still used, but the Exeter Hall is now the headquarters of this world-known organization. A convenient chapel for prayer-meetings and Bible-class instruction has been constructed; a fine reading-room and tea-room are across the main hall; a gymnasium is on the lower floor, and up on the second floor still remains that celebrated Hall (capable of holding three thousand) which has rung with the eloquence of Guthrie, Gavazzi, Gough, Beecher, Spurgeon and the most noted platformers of the last forty years.

Saturday afternoon was the most thoroughly enjoyable one I have spent in England. Mr. Hall drove me through South London to the beautiful villa of Mr. Spurgeon at Upper Norwood, near the Sydenham Crystal Palace. Mr. Spurgeon purchased it a year ago in exchange for his house at Clapham; and it is a rural paradise. The great preacher, with a jovial countenance came out of his door with both hands outstretched to give us welcome. Saturday afternoon is his holiday. For an hour he conducted us over his delightful grounds, and through his garden and conservatory, and then to a rustic arbor, where he entertained us with one of his racy talks which are as characteristic as his sermons. It may be no breach of privacy to give his estimate of the New Revision, which he pronounces a most valuable help to the study of the New Testament, but needing to be itself somewhat revised before it can come into universal use. He emphatically approves of the suggestions of the American revisers, and regrets that they had not been generally adopted by their English associates. This feeling is expressed by many eminent clergymen whom I meet here.

Mr. Spurgeon's study is a charming apartment opening out on his lawn; the view extends for twelve miles to Epsom Downs. His parlor too is lined with elegant volumes. He showed us with great glee a portfolio of caricatures of himself; and then by way of contrast, a series of translations of his sermons in various foreign tongues. His comely wife—for a long time a suffering invalid—presided at the table with grace and sweetness; their twin sons have already entered the ministry, one in London and the other now in New Zealand. It was six o'clock on Saturday when we bade him "good bye," and he assured us that he had not yet selected even the texts for his next day's discourses! "I shall go down in the garden presently," said he, "and arrange my morning discourse and choose a text for that in the evening; then to-morrow afternoon, before preaching, I will make an outline of the second one."

This is quite in conformity with his custom of preparing his discourses. He selects his text—often towards the close of Saturday—and devotes a half hour to arranging his heads or divisions, and jotting them down on a small bit of paper. Two of these outlines which he gave to me, are written on the backs of letter-envelopes. He told us that he "would rather be hung than attempt to write a sermon" and that he had never pre-composed a single sentence before entering the pulpit. "If I had a month given me to prepare a sermon" said he, "I would spend thirty days and twenty-three hours on something else, and in the last hour I would make the sermon. If I could not do it in an hour I could not do it in a month." This is certainly a remarkable mental habit and one which none of the rest of us had better try to imitate. But it must also be borne in mind that Mr. Spurgeon is a perpetual student. If he spends but a few moments in arranging a discourse, he spends much of each week in the most thorough and prayerful study of God's Word and in diligent reading of the richest writers (especially of the Puritan era), on theology and experimental religion. He is all the time filling up his cask, and when the emergency comes he has only to turn the spigot and *draw* It is not easy to exhaust a man who is always filling his head and heart from God's inexhaustible reservoir. Mr. Spurgeon was never more fertilizing in his ministry than he is at present; the two discourses which he delivered on the day after we visited him were up to his highest mark. I parted from him with fresh gratitude for seeing once more the man who, by tongue and pen, has brought the precious gospel to more souls than any man since the days of the Apostles.

XXVII.

DEAN STANLEY.

London, July, 25.

A WEEK ago yesterday, after the second service in Westminster Abbey, I went through to the door of the Deanery, to inquire after the Dean and to leave a message for him. No one felt any uneasiness about him, and a few moments previously Canon Farrar had told me that he was doing well. Just as we reached the door a bulletin was posted up that unfavorable symptoms had set in and grave apprehensions were entertained as to the issue. "Ah!" said Newman Hall to me, "our good friend, the Dean, is going to die." The next night, before the clock struck twelve, he was dead!

The whole nation was shocked and saddened to the heart; for on many accounts Dean Stanley was the best-loved man in the Church of England. He was the personal friend of the Queen, the tutor of the Prince Royal, the advocate of cordial fellowship among all denominations, the most simple, modest, and affectionate great man in the realm. His genius everybody admired; but his pure, sweet character everybody loved. So, for a week past great preparations have been making to give to the good Dean's remains such a burial ceremony as should bespeak the nation's affection and be worthy of the guardian of the great Abbey. The services really began yesterday morning, with an eloquent sermon by Canon Farrar, in which he extolled the moral courage of the Dean in standing by his honest convictions. In the afternoon I found the choir of the Abbey packed, and the adjoining transepts also. Presently Dr. Vaughan, the Dean of Llandaff and preacher in the Temple Church, ascended the pulpit so long occupied by his beloved friend, Stanley. Vaughan and Stanley were classmates at Rugby under Dr. Arnold, and their intimacy was very deep and cordial. It was a very trying occasion for Dr. Vaughan, and when he announced that he would preach on the very text that Dean Stanley had selected for his next discourse there he was very much overcome. It was a happy text for the hour: "Blessed are the pure in heart, for they shall see God." The famous preacher of the Temple is a fine, manly speaker and his style is almost perfect; so the discourse was a model funeral tribute. He happily said that Stanley had given perpetuity to Dr. Arnold's fame by writing his biography, and to Dr. Arnold's system of teaching by a living illustration of its beauty. In dwelling on the certainty of immortality, Dr. Vaughan exclaimed, with impassioned fervor: "Oh! what a wanton waste it were if such an intellect as Arthur Stanley's were destroyed!" The discourse was heard with deep emotion, and when it was through many of the audience, doubtless, said to themselves: "There stands the man to be the *next* Dean of Westminster."[1]

To-day, at four o'clock, the funeral service took place. Around the Abbey a vast multitude had assembled; not merely attracted by curiosity, for the Dean was a great favorite with the working classes. Thousands had applied for tickets of admission, and by the kindness of Canon Farrar and the timely attentions of one of the subordinates I secured an excellent seat in the front of the gallery over the Poet's Corner. It commanded a view of the whole ceremonies. Immediately below me was the tomb of Lord Macaulay, with its well-known inscription: "His body is buried in peace and his name liveth for evermore." Sir Charles Trevelyan, the brother-in-law of the great historian, was among the group of mourners. Beside Macaulay lie Campbell and Dickens, and upon them looks down the statue of Shakespeare.

[1] Dr. Vaughan afterwards declined the honor when offered to him.

The crowd in the Abbey was prodigious. Many of the guests climbed on the monuments, to witness the ceremonies. After long and patient waiting, we heard the funeral anthem sounding through the nave, and presently the procession entered. It contained the foremost living men of England. The heir to the throne marched in and occupied the pew of his old tutor, who was lying in the coffin before him. Upon the coffin were wreaths of "immortelles," and white flowers from the Westminster school boys, and a handful of Chinese roses from the Queen herself. The venerable Archbishop of Canterbury was in the line, Lord Shaftesbury, and Lord Houghton, and Tyndall, and Browning, and the Bishop of Peterborough. The coffin was borne by the same hands that had carried the Dean's beloved wife, Lady Augusta, to her burial, in Henry the Seventh's Chapel. It was set down before the pulpit in which the Dean had stood a few days before.

By the foot of the coffin the most conspicuous figure was William E. Gladstone.

He was called away before the service was over, and hastened to the House of Commons. (The pilot cannot leave the helm while the ship of state is off that Irish lee shore.) The funeral music to-day was solemn and sublime. Its rich strains swelled and rolled among the lofty arches with prodigious grandeur. Then the deep tones of the "Dead March" were heard, and the procession formed again. The body of ARTHUR STANLEY was taken up and tenderly carried over those historic stones, which he himself had trodden so often and so long. He was to be laid among the great, in his death.

With slow and measured tread, they bore him past the tomb of Dryden. Old Spenser, and Ben Jonson, and the author of the "Elegy in a Country Churchyard" were sleeping close by. A little further on, they passed the tomb of Edward the Confessor. The heir to the Confessor's throne was in the procession, and the descendants too of many a great warrior who lay in silent stone effigy on those monuments. Gradually the line passed on and on among the columns, until it entered the door of Henry the Seventh's Chapel and disappeared from my view.

As I looked at the dark-palled coffin, with its fragrant burden of flowers, vanishing out of sight I felt a peculiar grief; for,—wide as were our differences of opinion on some vital points of doctrine—the Dean had been to me a very kind and beloved friend. I had broken bread with him in his hospitable home. I had enjoyed with him a memorable visit to the Jerusalem Chamber; and on his last day in America he had gone with me to Greenwood and had asked me to conduct him to the grave of Dr. Edward Robinson, and to the spot where slumbers my own beloved child. A few years ago, a correspondence passed between us which only heightened my esteem for both his meekness, and his manliness. Amid all the adulations of court and aristocracy he never lost the devout simplicity of a minister of the living God. A gentler, sweeter, and more unselfish heart I have seldom known; and no man has been laid to his rest amid more sincere lamentations, in all this realm, for many a year than Arthur Penrhyn Stanley. Of him too it may be said that his body is buried in peace, but his name doth live on for evermore.

XXVIII.

THE DRINK-QUESTION IN MANY LANDS.

London, July 27.

"KEEP your eye upon the drink-question wherever you go" was a counsel which I did not need, for I have always made this a matter of careful observation when travelling in foreign lands. A confirmed teetotaler from my youth I shall return home with increased convictions that the practice of total abstinence from all intoxicants is a wise practice for all ages, climes, and conditions. Some Americans who do not habitually use wines or brandies at home, become so alarmed at the idea that the water in certain countries will work them mischief that they do not risk the experiment of using it, and begin at once to take a little wine—or more—"for their stomach's sake." Having none of these imaginary fears, I have adhered to that honest wholesome beverage that the Creator has provided for every animate creature that flies the heavens, walks the earth, or swims the sea. On every steamer and in nearly every hotel a "wine list" has been placed before me. But I have steadily adhered to beverages guiltless of alcohol, and have found that pure water—whether it were the Nile-water of Egypt, or the rain-water of Jerusalem, or the acqueduct-water of Athens, or the water of every land from the Mediterranean to the Baltic, was perfectly adapted to my constitution—and by-laws also. I am not alone in this testimony; for I had two fellow-travellers in the Orient who had adhered to their teetotalism in India as rigidly as they did in Palestine. But I did not discover that totalabstainers travel "in regiments."

In Egypt and throughout the Levant the conscientious Mussulmen obey the restrictions of the Koran and avoid the use of wine. Some of the looser sort break the rules of the Prophet; a gentleman in Jaffa told me that there was an increasing tendency there to tippling. In the main, the Moslems are abstinent. The Copts in Egypt frequently use "arrack"—a spirituous liquor distilled from grapes, or fermented rice or palm-juice, and at their evening meals often drink to excess. The first town in the East which I found to be cursed with ubiquitous dram-shops and drenched in strong drink was Port Said. That is a sea-port, conglomerated of all nationalities, and is an exotic on Egyptian soil.

In Palestine and Syria the people (who are not Mohammedans)—almost universally use the native wines, which are abundant, cheap, and contain but a small percentage of alcohol. Some of the poorer Jews in Jerusalem, who are unable to purchase wine for the Passover, are in the habit of boiling raisins and extracting a simple unfermented drink which they use at the Paschal feast. They always ask a blessing on it as "*the fruit of the vine.*" The mild drink thus made will not keep long, and it is not much used as a beverage. Several syrups are made from the grape, which are brought on the table as maple-syrup is in Vermont or molasses on the breakfast-tables of boarding-schools. There is very little drunkenness in Palestine. Bishop Barclay told me that the only time at which the Jews in Jerusalem get exhilarated is at the Feast of Purim. Then it is regarded as a meritorious act to get so "fuddled" that a man does not know the difference between "blessed be Haman!" and "cursed be Mordecai!"

At Ephesus, I saw a company of Greeks and Syrians carousing in a dram-shop, and the Greeks throughout the Orient are sometimes hard drinkers. After I reached Innspruck and began to encounter the social usages, I. soon saw that I was regarded with some astonishment because I did not, at the table, order either wine or beer. The consumption of beer in Austria, Germany, and Denmark, is almost as general as the use of cold-water in American farm-houses. I saw only one person intoxicated, and that was in the streets of Prague,—where a well-dressed man was reeling on the sidewalk. But because I observed no public exhibitions of drunkenness it does not follow that drunkenness does not exsist in Germany. On the contrary, there is a great deal of intemperance among the Germans; and the enormous use of beer not only involves an enormous waste of money among the working classes, but also leads to the use of distilled liquors. I learn that last year a noteworthy debate touching this subject occurred in the German Parliament at Berlin. It was on a proposition to tax the retailing of beer, wine, and stronger liquors. The proposition was made by the Government, and, as the Finance Minister said, not so much for the purpose of raising revenue, as of restricting the sale of beverages, the excessive use of which was injuring the health and morals of the people, and creating amongst the most intelligent and thoughtful observers no little apprehension concerning the future prosperity of the State.

In the German cities the beer-gardens are not only associated with a fearful desecration of the Sabbath, but in too many cases, the beer-shop is the fruitful source of the worst forms of profligacy. A well-informed writer for *Scribner's Monthly* declares that—

"The curse of Berlin is its ten thousand beer and wine cellars, hidden away in subterranean retreats, where security from the public gaze is an inducement to a visit on the part of those who would hesitate to enter them if open to general view. Many of these are the retreats of the lowest species of vice and degradation, and the resorts of criminals in all stages of depravity. The uninitiated would neither find nor suspect the existence of half of them, and he who would study the subject worthily needs a trusty policeman as guide and protector."

As I went northward I found the popular beverages becoming more strongly alcoholic. Until about twenty-five years ago Sweden was cursed by a frightful amount of drunkenness, especially among the lower classes. The most common Swedish liquor is called "Bran-vin" and is a powerful intoxicant distilled from potatoes. The first step towards reform was the passage of a "Licensing act" in 1855; this act abolished domestic distillation, imposed heavy license-fees and allowed the parochial authorities or the town-councils to fix the number of liquor-shops. It even allowed them to prohibit tippling-houses entirely. The result of the passage of this law was to reduce the annual product of Branvin from 26,000,000 gallons to 6,900,000! Under the act, the traffic in ardent spirits was much restricted in many parishes, and was not licensed at all in several localities. Its chief results were seen in the rural districts. While this law has vastly curtailed the sale and use of intoxicants, yet in the city of Gothenburg—the chief sea-port—the drink-traffic went forward with scarcely any perceptible hindrance. The City Council accordingly decided that drinking-houses should no longer be managed by private individuals for the sake of personal profit, but by a Company (or "Bolag"), and that all the net profits of the sale of spirits should be paid over to the city treasury. A "Bolag" was organized in 1865, and a charter was granted them by the Government.

This "Gothenburg system" of license is now, in full force, in several of the large towns of Sweden. Under this system the whole sale of liquor in a city is committed to a joint-stock company, who decide on the number of drinking-houses and pay the salaries of the venders. After a small dividend has been declared to the share-holders, all the remainder of the profits from the sales are paid into the city treasury. The number of dram-shops under this method is greatly reduced; in Upsala, with a population of eighteen thousand, there are only seventeen. An effort is now being made by the friends of temperance to have the dram-shops closed on Saturday evenings, on holidays, and on the whole of the Sabbath. They are only open now on Sunday for two or three hours. The most intelligent persons with whom I conversed generally state that the "Gothenburg system" works many good results. It limits the number of drinking-houses; it allows no inducement to the liquor-seller to sell for personal profit; it forbids the sale of intoxicants to an intoxicated person, and forbids also any one to get drunk "on the premises." If there is to be any license at all, this is probably the best license system ever invented. Its cardinal defect is that it legalizes the dram-shop, and opens a doorway of deadly temptation. The best people in Sweden therefore, are now enlisted in moral efforts to persuade their countrymen to abstain from strong drink entirely. Under the leadership of such devoted Christians as Professor Truvè, Rev. Mr. Lagergren, Col. Broady, and other of like spirit, the total-abstinence reform is making rapid progrēss. I found that in Upsala a single society of teetotalers numbered over seven hundred members.

Two very palpable principles seem to prevail in regard to the use of alcoholic stimulants. The one is that the character of the popular beverages, varies according to the *climate*. In warm countries, such as Egypt, Palestine, Syria, and southern Italy, those beverages are of a milder character. As I went northward I found the potations of the people growing more intensely alcoholic. The thirst for intoxicants seems to go up as the thermometer goes down. Had I pursued my journeyings as far as Siberia I should have discovered that the native tribes are addicted to eating a peculiar fungus plant called "muk-a-moor" which is a violent narcotic and which completely shatters the nervous system. Although the sale of this terrible intoxicant is prohibited by Russian law, yet so eager is the appetite of the Siberians for it that they readily offer the most valuable furs to the Russian traders who will smuggle it into their possession.

If the use of alcoholic drinks varies according to climate it also varies according to *race*. The Semitic and the Latin races are content with milder potations. The Saxons, the Scandinavians and the Celts have appetites for "bottled lightning." It is not a pleasant thing to say, but the most hideous drunkenness that I have yet encountered is to be found in Britain and in Ireland. London alone must contain more habitual drunkards than does all the native population of the Levant. This loathsome vice meets you at every turn in the eastern and southern sections of the metropolis; it penetrates into the "West End," and numbers its victims in every tier of society. One of the most offensive features of London life is that strong drink is not only sold most commonly by *women* in the dram shops, but that women are so widely the victims of the drink. Not only in the Strand but on many other thoroughfares I saw scores of females around the counters of the gin-palaces. Sometimes husbands and wives go in together for their dram. This terrible traffic is at its worst on Sabbath evenings! When riding home from church, my friend Mr. Hall would frequently say to me "let us count the gin-palaces that are open on this street," and we would find a dozen within the distance of an hundred rods. All through the Lord's day hundreds of churches and chapels are opened to preach salvation by the Cross; at night ten thousand doorways of perdition are flung open to preach damnation by the dram. What is true of London is measurably true of all the large towns of England, Scotland and Ireland.

Within the last three or four years the indefatigable labor of the advocates of temperance are beginning to make some tangible impression upon this monster evil. Four years ago the sale of ardent spirits and beer amounted to 115,000,000 pounds sterling annually. It has been steadily reduced (in spite of increase of population) until last year it amounted to 106,000,000. Among the middle and higher classes, the practice of entire abstinence is making headway. Such influential men in the Church of England as Bishop Lightfoot (of Durham), the Bishop of Exeter, Canon Farrar, and Canon Basil Wilberforce, are throwing the weight of their powerful influence in favor of it. Dr. B. W. Richardson, by his able physiological writings and addresses, is arousing the medical fraternity. Temperance hospitals have been established and are working successfully. Coffee-houses are being opened in all the towns as an antidote to the gin-palace. Sir Wilfred Lawson and his United Kingdom Alliance are pushing the agitation for "Local option" with increasing vigor. The National Temperance League are flooding the kingdom with their volumes and tracts. Many of the most influential Dissenting pulpits are becoming most pronounced in their advocacy of the temperance movement. And it would not be an act of justice to close this extended letter without saying that our countryman Mr. Joseph Cook has—during the past twelvemonth—struck some powerful blows which have produced a deep impression throughout the kingdom.

XXIX.

EXCURSIONS IN ENGLAND.

London, August 2.

IT is impossible to chronicle all the pleasant experiences of the past week, but I will attempt what Willis used to call a "hurry-graph" of a few of them. On Tuesday I took a run down to Devonshire, which many regard as the garden of England. I halted at Salisbury for a look at the Cathedral, the chief glory of which is the spire—four hundred feet high. The Bishop's Palace is a delicious piece of old architecture encased in greenery. A few miles north of Salisbury is Stonehenge; and beyond it stretch the Downs, over which Hannah More's "Shepherd" drove his flocks. That charming story ought to be revived into popularity.

On entering Devonshire we passed through Axminster, a most beautiful town, but now producing only a small number of the carpets, which have made the place so famous. Then came Honiton, equally famous for its laces, which are made by young women, by a slow manual process. Exeter, the capital of the county, stands in a region of enchanting loveliness; just out of the town is Sir Stafford Northcote's mansion, and in the heart of the town is the Cathedral, six hundred years old.

The building is rather long for its height, but the nave is so rich in branching tracery that to walk beneath the architectural foliage is like a walk through a grove of Egyptian palms. On one side is the "Minstrel's Gallery," the carved front of which represents twelve angels who are playing upon trumpets, horns, and various musical instruments. That is a choir that ought never to give pastors or music-committees any trouble. The front of the Cathedral is very low, and thoroughly blackened by coal-smoke, and antiquity; yet the whole front is covered by the "Grandison screen," a piece of stone work which is fashioned into columns, and niches. and multitudinous statues of saints, and kings and heroes of the faith. Up in the north transept is a remarkable astronomical clock, on which are inscribed the very suggestive words, "Pereunt et imputantur." It would have been music to the ears of the poet Gray to have heard the curfew-bell tolled each night from the ancient towers. The sounds are like echoes from the far-gone past.

From Exeter I had a pleasant ride to Wells in Somersetshire; a farmer who sat by me pointing out the various mansions and telling me how many of them were changing owners, and how large a purchase of land had lately been made by a rich Londoner who wears the rather uncommon name of "Smith." As I entered the city of Wells, I was reminded of the old chorister who, pitch-pipe in hand, used to call out that word before he began a favorite tune much sung in the church of my boyhood. My chief object in visiting the quiet little city was to see its Cathedral—which was built five hundred years ago on the site of a church founded by King Ina in the year 704. There are two superb features of this Cathedral which are not surpassed anywhere in the kingdom. The one is its magnificent west front which is two hundred and thirty-five feet in length, and is divided into several distinct compartments by projecting buttresses. All of these compartments and buttresses are swarming with statues which number, large and small, about six hundred. The object of these statues, it is said, is to represent the order of the subjects in the "Te Deum." The lower tier illustrates the line, "The glorious company of the Apostles praise Thee." The next tier represents, "The goodly army of the Prophets praise Thee." Then comes the "noble army of martyrs," and so on upward until the highest tiers close with a sculptured picture of the Resurrection of the dead and the Day of Judgment. It is a grand conception of sacred art, and is carried out with the most elaborate and conscientious detail. I stood on the velvet greensward before the edifice, and read, as in a huge stone book, the history of human redemption by the gospel of the cross.

The other superior feature of this cathedral is the choir. When I looked through its exquisitely light and delicate Gothic arches at the gorgeous stained glass of the Lady Chapel behind it, the amazing beauty overpowered me. It was worthy to be placed alongside of the feats of delicacy in finish wrought by the Greek builders of the Erectheum. From the Bishop of Wells, good Thomas Ken, came the familiar morning and evening hymns, with their matchless doxology—

"Praise God from whom all blessings flow."

How few of the millions who sing those lines, ever heard the name of their author! It is a striking coincidence that the finest hymns in the English language should have been composed in those southern counties that stretch along the Channel. Toplady wrote the "Rock of Ages," and Charlotte Elliott her hymn "Just as I am" in Devonshire. Henry Lyte the author of "Abide with me" lived in the same county. Charles Wesley gave birth to "Jesus lover of my soul" and Perronet to the hymn "All hail the power of Jesus' name," in that same poetic belt of the south of England. Isaac Watts penned his first hymn at Southampton, opposite to the Isle of Wight.

One of my pleasant excursions this week was to Kingston Hill, and Richmond Park on the Thames; under the oaks of this park the Queen gave a home to the veteran Earl Russell in his closing days. England takes good care of her old servants. She stows them away in various good quarters just as she moors the hulk of the famous flag-ship "Victory" in the quiet waters of Portsmouth harbor. She also treasures very carefully the autographs, the manuscripts and other relics of her renowned authors and heroes.

In the British Museum the other day I saw the "Elegy in a Country Churchyard," in the neat and delicate hand of its author, Thomas Gray. Close by was a page of Lord Macaulay's History of England, a large foolscap sheet written over in large, bold hand, and completely covered with erasures and interlineations. This shows that it was Macaulay's habit to write down rapidly whatever came into his mind; then he went over it with corrections and alterations. The same thing is observable in Dickens's manuscript of *David Copperfield* and *Oliver Twist* and *Chuzzlewit*—all of which are preserved entire in the South Kensington Museum. There is not one line that is not blotched over with corrections. I read with intense interest an original letter of Robert Burns, in which he thanks Mrs. Dunlop, "for your favorable opinion of my 'Tam o' Shanter.'" Little did the poor ploughman dream that after an hundred years the world would know Tam o' Shanter by heart.

Among all the rare and precious curiosities in the two Museums, none delighted me more than two letters of Oliver Cromwell. They were almost entirely in Scripture language, and the spelling is almost as bad as Queen Elizabeth's. In the rough draft of her speech to Parliament good Queen Bess tells them that "the eeys of all lokers on have been blinded through too cessions." The woman who spelled in that style boasted of her scholastic attainments! London is fast being robbed of its ancient structures. Temple Bar is gone; Milton's and Shakespeare's houses are gone; and Surrey Chapel is soon to be pulled down. Yesterday I crossed the Thames to explore "St. Saviour's Church, Southwark," which comes next to Westminster Abbey in historic interest. In the Lady-chapel, Bloody Mary's brutal Bishop Gardiner condemned Protestants to death, and on the memorial windows are the names of Bishop Hooper, burned at Gloucester, and of John Rogers, burned at Smithfield. In one corner of the church John Gower, the contemporary poet with Chaucer, lies buried;

and under the pavement sleep Philip Massinger and Edmond Shakespeare, the youngest brother of the immortal dramatist. Quaint epitaphs abound. One brass plate records in pompous phrase the wonderful qualities of a maiden *ten* years old, who was "none-such for piety and virtue," and who is now "maid of honor to the King in Heaven!" No other metal but *brass* could contain such inflated nonsense as that. Shakespeare's Globe Theatre stood close by that ancient church, but has given place to a brewery. Chaucer's "Tabard Inn," was about half a mile away, and that has given place to a warehouse. London will soon be as modern as New York.

Yesterday I hunted up one delightful bit of antiquity that is as yet untouched—and that is St. Giles' Church, Cripple-gate, near the Bank of England. It is a beautiful church, and in its green yard stands a Roman tower built nineteen centuries ago! Under the floor of this dear old church lies "John Milton, author of *Paradise Lost.*" I went to the altar-rail, and knelt down with deep emotion, for I was on the spot where Oliver Cromwell knelt when he was married to his Huguenot wife. In the vestry, I read the record of his marriage, and of Milton's interment. This city is fairly peopled with statues. Sir Robert Peel's handsome figure is at the end of Cheapside, and in the open court near Westminster Abbey, and in the Abbey itself. They cannot pay too high honors to the king of parliamentarians and the honest statesman. Sir John Franklin has a touching memorial near Carlton House. King Billy the sailor has a statue too, although his place in history is scanty enough. One of the most spirited pieces of art is that superb figure of Richard the Lion-hearted,* who bestrides his bronze horse in front of the Victoria Tower at Wesminster as if he were a gallant Knight set for Her Majesty's defence.

One thing surprises me; and that is that

---

* A representation of this statue fronts the title-page of this volume.

RICHARD COEUR-DE-LION
and the
PALACE OF WESTMINSTER.

FRONTISPIECE.

while London abounds in monuments to England's celebrities, it does not contain a single monument to the two greatest rulers England has had for three centuries—Oliver Cromwell and King William of Orange! In the mean time stone enough has been piled up in various places in honor of good Prince Albert to build a church.

During this week an International Convention of Young Men's Christian Associations is holding its sessions at Exeter Hall. This famous old edifice in the Strand—whose walls have echoed to the eloquence of the foremost preachers, missionaries and reformers of this century—has lately been purchased by the London Y. M. C. A. Its Secretary, Mr. W. Hind Smith, is a powerful organizer—and his wife, whom I once knew as Miss Wilson of Sherwood Hall, is the most untiring female philanthropist in the city. We must come to England in order to learn systematic thoroughness in managing benevolent operations. America excels in effervescent spurts, and dashes; John Bull beats us in the long and steady pull. If there could be a combination of American enthusiasm with British thoroughness and hold-on-a'iveness, we would have the ideal system of efficient Reforms.

This Convention is well attended, and its sessions are spirited and profitable. Our country is represented by its two distinguished workers—the Hon. William E. Dodge, who will speak at the public meeting to-morrow evening, and Mr. John Wanamaker of Philadelphia, who led the prayer-meeting on Saturday evening. Mr. McBurney of New York, and Rev. Dr. Newman of New York, are also present, with about twenty others.

Last evening the Lord Mayor and Lady Mayoress gave a grand reception to the delegates in the Mansion House. The present Mayor, Hon. Mr. McArthur, is a member of Parliament, a rich merchant, and a devout Methodist. At seven o'clock, a large company of us found ourselves in the superb central hall of the Mansion House where His

Honor received us in official state. He wore his scarlet robes and gold chain; upon his right hand stood an officer attired in black robe and the traditional cap, and bearing an immense sword; on his left hand was a similar functionary bearing the huge gilded lace. To the Lord Mayor and his portly Mayoress we were each introduced; and in the company I observed the Earl of Shaftesbury, the Hon. Samuel Gurney, Bevan Braithwaite (the leader of the Orthodox Quakers, and one of the best men in England), Mr. Arthur Kinnaird, Mr. Matheson, and other eminent Christian merchants and bankers. A procession was formed, and we marched into the magnificent "Egyptian" Banquet Hall —one of the most gorgeous apartments in London, and looking like a quotation from Windsor Palace. It is lined with lofty gilded columns and statuary, and its frescoed ceiling is at least seventy feet from the floor. Upon a dais at the end of this palatial hall sat the Lord Mayor, and his five hundred guests were seated before him. The Earl of Shaftesbury made a ringing speech, which was received with boisterous enthusiasm. Addresses were made by foreign delegates —the Hon. Mr. Dodge responding handsomely for America. Mr. Russell Sturgis, of Boston, and Mr. George Williams the founder of the Association took a prominent part. Altogether it was a splendid affair, and we all went home concluding that our generous Christian host was indeed the *Lord's* Mayor; for he is using his eminent station and influence directly for the glory of God.

London, August 6.

This is my last day in this colossal city, which always has such a fascination for me that I am loath to leave it. London is a volume of a thousand leaves; no man living has yet read every page. Yesterday I was in the neighborhood of the General Post-office in St. Martin's le Grand, and I threaded my way through several narrow streets into Nettleton Court. In "No. 2" of that narrow court John Wesley was converted; for he tells us that there he first tasted of the love of God. In that little dingy brick house—where I found a poor woman washing clothes—Methodism was born. It is not a very long walk from that obscure nook to City Road Chapel in which Wesley held his most frequent services, and beside which he now lies buried. I told the woman at the wash-tub that when the Ecumenical Council of Methodism comes off in September she might expect an inundation of visitors. Quite sure I am that the American delegates will hunt out the spot, for our countrymen are keener on the scent for historical relics than any other class of visitors to England. On the Sabbaths they constitute a large element in the congregations at Mr. Spurgeon's Tabernacle, and at Westminster Abbey. At the public meeting held in Exeter Hall by the "World's Convention of Young Men's Christian Associations" on Wednesday evening, many Americans were present. The Hon. William E. Dodge spoke briefly; Dr. John Hall was in the audience, with President Magoun of

Iowa University, and several delegates from New York. When I introduced the name of our President into my address, it did our hearts good to see the audience rise up and cheer vociferously. The Earl of Shaftesbury, who presided, afterwards read a telegram from Mrs. Garfield, at which there was another shout. Herr Klug from Elberfeld, Germany, delivered an eloquent speech; but the hero of the evening was the veteran Lord Shaftesbury, whose appearance always calls forth great enthusiasm. He is over eighty years of age, but as erect as a Norway pine, and he has but few gray hairs on his honored head. It is owing to both climate and physical constitution—as well as to temperament—that Englishmen preserve their full vigor to such an extreme age. Lord Palmerston was once asked, "when is a man in his prime?" and he drily replied—"oh, about seventy-nine; but I am past my prime, for I am just eighty." This English atmosphere is very favorable to consecutive hard work, both out doors and in. It is not subject to the violent extremes of the climate in our Northern states—a climate that has been wittily satirized as one in which 'during the summer, butter may be sold by the pint and during the winter milk may be sold by the pound."

I spent a delightful evening this week at the house of Bevan Braithwaite, who is one of the most earnest warm-hearted Christians I have ever met. He practices law during the week, and preaches in his Quaker meeting-house on "first day," and finds time to make himself one of the most profound Bible scholars in London. He brought out his Septuagint and Codex Vaticanus, and entertained us with a most learned discussion of the merits and the demerits of the New Revision. After hearing his opinions and those of Mr. Spurgeon, I feel confident that the Revision will not be cordially and generally adopted in England. Friend Braithwaite is one of the directors of the British and Foreign Bible Society, and for a layman, is a master of biblical criticism. He feels as do many others, that it would have been prudent for the Revisers to have submitted their work to the outside public in a tentative way for free criticism, before they finally adopted it. For myself I have had but little opportunity to examine the Westminster Revision, and while I like it exceedingly, I believe that it would have been improved if the Revisers had called in thirty or forty cultivated Christian laymen, and consulted their judgment on several points. God's Word is also the people's book.

I am happy to learn that this Westminster version is received with so much favor in America, for whatever be its defects it is a vast improvement upon the much more defective Version of King James's translators.

No city in the world can show such a band of Christian philanthropists, or such organizations of benevolence, as London. It needs them all, and tenfold more; for its wickedness is colossal. Every Sabbath evening ten thousand dram-shops are in full blast; the great majority of the drink-sellers are young women! And among the crowds pouring into these doorways of perdition, the women are almost as numerous as the men! There are over forty thousand women who make a trade of their profligacy. In such thoroughfares as the Strand and around the "Aquarium," they swarm every evening in regiments. It almost makes even New York seem virtuous, to go through certain portions of this great British Babylon by gas-light. But against this immense tide of vice and poverty and debauchery, God's people are making head as bravely and steadily as they can. There are four hundred city missionaries, scores of "Bible-readers" and lady visitors; Mr. Noble is working zealously among the degraded slums of Hoxton, Mr. Barnardo in another quarter, and the Mildmay Park missionaries in many quarters. They are all achieving blessed results; but the greatest single power in London is Charles H. Spurgeon, with his mighty pulpit and his staff of trained laborers.

One day I have spent at Canterbury. That is the original fountain-head of English civilization, culture and Christianity. There St. Augustine preached to the Saxons, and Anselm wielded his crosier. An university was planted there while Cambridge was still a fen, and Oxford was still a forest. My companions to the ancient town were President Magoun of Iowa university and Rev. Julius Read; we went by the Southeastern Railway, through Chiselhurst and Tunbridge. By the roadside stands the old manor-house in which the beautiful Anne Boleyn was born, and whence she was called to her dizzy and dangerous elevation as the wife of a royal brute.

Canterbury is very old, and is yet very well scoured up, so that its antiquity betrays no rust or shabbiness. Through streets lined with small houses of one or two stories, we made our way to the venerable Cathedral. It is of immense length—five hundred and twenty feet—and some of the perspectives in the interior are of marvellous beauty.

A walk around its outer wall and cloisters was almost a quarter of a mile; it took us by some grand old Norman arches, and the cosey ivy-covered house in which Dean Stanley lived when he was Canon of Canterbury. There is a window also which he placed in one of the transepts as a memorial of his tour to the Holy Land.

The Choir of the Cathedral is of great size and splendor. Just beyond it is the tomb of that royal model of true chivalry, Edward the Black Prince; above the effigy of the hero, are suspended the shield he bore, and the coat he wore at Crecy and Poitiers. On the opposite side is the tomb of Henry the Fourth. But no king or warrior that sleeps beneath that Cathedral had to me a tithe of the interest which I have felt for the good DEAN ALFORD who preached there for many years. There is a rich stained glass memorial window which bears his fragrant name. But he is not buried within the Cathedral walls. He selected his own resting-place in the little crowded churchyard of "St. Martin's."

That is the oldest Church in England. It is not over thirty feet long, and its low square tower is wrapped around with ivy. On the stone floor of its chancel it is claimed that Augustine stood, twelve centuries ago! In the ancient Runic font by the door he baptized Ethelbert the Saxon; that church was old when William the Conqueror landed in Britain. In front of the church stand two venerable yew-trees; beneath one of these trees is a plain, simple tomb that bears the beloved name of "Henry Alford." On the end of the tomb is the celebrated inscription composed by the Dean himself—"Deversorium viatoris Hierosolymam proficientis," "The inn of a traveller bound to J rusalem." Of all the hundreds of inscriptions that I have read during my wanderings, this one is the most exquisite; nor have I stood by the grave of a purer or a more leal hearted minister of God.

XXX.

A RUN INTO WALES.

Adelphi Hotel, Liverpool, Aug. 12.

I LEFT London on Saturday, my last evening being passed under the roof of my friend, Hon. Arthur Kinnaird. Both he and his father, Lord Kinnaird, are among the "staff" of the Earl of Shaftesbury in conducting Christian campaigns of usefulness. No city in the world has a nobler body of practica' philanthropists than London has in the persons of the two Kinnairds, Samuel Morley, William Hind Smith, Matthew Hodder, John Taylor, T. B. Smithies, and their coadjutors. The Earl of Aberdeen is also becoming prominent in evangelical activities.

My route hither was by the Midland Railway through the ravishing regions of Derbyshire—such as Matlock, Rowsley, and Darleydale. Chatsworth and Haddon Hall were out of sight from the train, but we did not need them to complete the picture of luxuriant loveliness. If a visitor to England can explore only two counties, let him select Devonshire and Derbyshire. The crops are fine this season, and the gold of the wheatfields blends with the green of the meadows and the hedge-rows. For quite too many of my visits hitherward, I have been cheated out of a sight of Wales. So I came to Liverpool in season for a brief run through the four northern counties of the old Principality.

The mountains of Wales are picturesque, though not lofty enough to be sublime. But old, Christopher North said that the most beautiful spots on this earth are the Welsh valleys. He must have had in his mind the valleys of Dolgelly and Llangollen, and the Cressford vale that lies close to Cheshire. Again and again I said to myself. "Well, *this* is the gem of all that I have seen yet"; but my casket of memory is full of gems, each one differing from the rest in some peculiar glory. At this season of the year North Wales is crowded with Londoners, with whom it is a favorite summer resort. Canon Farrar is at Penraenmawr, recruiting from a year's work that had quite worn him down. If the suffrages of Americans could be counted, this brilliant and brave man would be appointed to the vacant Deanery of Westminster. The choice is supposed to lie between Dr. Butler of Harrow, and the Bishop of Manchester. But it will be a long time ere there is another Dean Stanley. Before I left London, I went to pay a last visit to his grave in Henry the Seventh's Chapel; it was still covered with wreaths and flowers from many loving hearts. He lived the life of a true man; he now sleeps the sweet sleep of a little child.

But I am wandering from Wales. I found the northern coast lined with picturesque villages, and cottages nestled in their greeneries. We caught glimpses of ancient Conway Castle—out of whose ruined windows six centuries of history are peering—and of modern Penrhyn Castle, whose lordly owner is also the owner of the largest slate-quarries in the country. I halted at Caernarvon to explore the famous Castle, which ranks next to Warwick in extent and interest. The first King Edward built it about 1284; the first Prince of Wales (the unhappy Edward II. of England) was born there.

It is a kingly pile, five hundred feet in length. A whole regiment could be encamped in tents, within its ample walls. I climbed to the battlements of its "Eagle Tower," and got a wide view of the island of Anglesey, and the distant Menai Bridge, which the genius of Stephenson constructed forty years ago. The contrast between Caernarvon Castle—with its frowning battlements, gloomy keeps and belligerent looking heads carved around the towers—and that noble highway for traffic and travel showed the essential difference between the thirteenth century and the nineteenth. The only occupant of the stately castle, which once rang with the trumpets of armed knights, is a shrewd Welshman who sells photographs and keeps a register for Yankee tourists to inscribe their names.

From Caernarvon I went up to the village of Llanberris, under the shadow of old Snowdon. At the "Dolbadarn Inn" were parties of tourists who had just ascended this monarch of the Welsh mountains; others were arriving by four-horse coaches from Bettys-wy-Coed and Beddgelert and Festiniog. The most striking sight at Llanberris was the huge mountain of slate, up which the various quarries ascended like a colossal flight of stairs. Those quarries give employment to about 3,000 persons. Many of them come from a long distance on Monday morning, and return home on Saturday evening. If any one wishes to see the Welsh peasantry in their primitive dress and style of living, he must go off from the thoroughfares: for railways and fashionable travel have revolutionized the rural life of those districts that are now haunted by summer tourists. If any one also wishes to know whence came all the

Joneses and Robertses and Evanses so familiar in America, let him go to Wales; those three popular surnames are on half the signs in the streets. I also saw an abundance of Williams, with a sprinkling of Owens and Griffiths.

I spent my first night at Port Madoc, a small village surrounded with bare mist-covered hills. The word "Temperance" inscribed over the doors of two inns, and of several groceries was a cheering indication of the spread of wholesome principles in the land of Christmas Evans and Howell Harris. There is not probably a country on the globe that contains a more God-fearing peasantry than Wales. The next morning I was in the train by six o'clock, and soon caught a glimpse of gray old Harlech Castle planted on a lofty steep. This is another of Edward's strongholds and was captured by the most famous of Welsh heroes, Owen Glendower. It is the theme of the most popular song of the Cambrians. Had time permitted I would fain have lingered for a week in the enchanting vale of Dolgelly, feasting on its verdure that "a Shenstone might have envied." To the Welshman in foreign lands, the recollection of such an exquisite spot as Dolgelly, with its silver-footed stream and the gentle outline of its hills and the sheen of its emerald grass must be a memory to kindle the pangs of homesickness. A level monotonous prairie in Nebraska or a smoky iron-manufacturing town in Pennsylvania must seem to him rather prosaic in the comparison.

The most interesting spot to me was Bala, in the beautiful valley of the Dee. It is the site of a Calvinistic Theological School of fifty students under the presidency of Dr. Lewis Edwards. But it owes its chief fame to that apostolic man, Rev. Thomas Charles, the real originator of the British and Foreign Bible Society, and all kindred organizations. Mr. Charles was the pastor of a Calvinistic Methodist church in Bala, and very active in promoting religious schools and study of the Scriptures. But Bibles were scarce and very dear. One day when he was questioning one of his Sunday-school girls, she said, "The weather has been so bad this week that I could not get to see a Bible." He found that the poor girl had to walk seven miles every week to get a look at a copy of God's Word! He determined at once to go to London, and induce rich Christians there to organize a society to supply the Scriptures to the people of Wales. The thing was done, and it proved to be the seed-corn out of which grew the greatest Bible Society on the globe.

About a mile from Bala, we passed the good man's grave, under a clump of yew-trees on the banks of a beautiful little lake. On reaching the railway station, we crossed the River Dee by the "Mwn-wyl-y-Llyn Bridge." (I defy any one but a Welshman to pronounce that name, or the name of a village called Ynyscymbanarn!) Up in the town I came upon the chapel in which Mr. Charles once preached—or rather the new edifice that takes its place. In front of the tasteful edifice is a fine statue of the man himself in pure white marble. Upon the pedestal is a bas-relief representing him distributing Bibles among his neighbors. In the neighboring parsonage I had a pleasant interview with the Rev. Mr. Edwards—a son of the College President, and a grandson of Thomas Charles. It must be an inspiration to him to get a look at his noble ancestor's countenance in marble every time he walks past to his pulpit.

From Bala I came to lovely Llangollen, and thence past Chirk and Cressford valleys to Chester and Liverpool. Here ends my happy, eventful, and instructive five months' pilgrimage. Since leaving home, I have travelled more than nine thousand miles. I have seen some of the most famous cities on the globe. Of these, the five that have interested me most deeply have been Cairo, Jerusalem, Athens, Stockholm, and London. This last named city is a kingdom of itself. It has been permitted me to study the progress of Christ's cause and glorious Gospel, and to hold pleasant converse with many honored missionaries, ministers and philanthropists. The goodness and mercy of God, and the kindness of many friends, have followed me at every step. But I can honestly say that after beholding all the Old World could show me, I care more to see the faces of that beloved flock who sent me on this trip to the Orient, than any object this side of the ocean. Towards them I set my face to-morrow, and then "Point *home* my country's flag of stars." When I see that ensign at the mast-head of the steamer Algeria, my heart will leap like the roe. America is never so welcome to an American as when he returns thither from a foreign land. And if I am permitted to set foot on its dear soil, I can chant the hymn of the Pilgrims to Plymouth Rock:

> ' Who thought on England's fields of green,
> Nor wept that ocean rolled between;
> But praised the Lord—the Lord their Guide—
> Who brought them o'er the swelling tide."

XXXI.

HOMEWARD.

Steamship "Algeria," August 22.

MY summer passage homeward was as pleasant as a good ship, good weather, and good company can make it. On the evening before our departure I visited the noble building of the Young Men's Christian Association—whose corner-stone was laid by our American Evangelist Mr. Moody. There is an extensive suite of apartments, such as reading-room, class-rooms, parlor, gymnasium, etc., all very attractive to the young men of Liverpool for whom it was reared. Looking into the lecture-hall, I found a social meeting of ladies and gentlemen with Mr. Alexander Guthrie (a son of the celebrated Edinburgh orator) in the chair. In the course of an off-hand address I took occasion to urge the greater development of the laity in the spiritual work of the churches. In the English and Scotch churches the private members are not called out into various activities as much as they are in our American congregations. For example, it is the custom with us to commit the weekly devotional meetings to the management of the lay-officers—the elders, or deacons, or class-leaders or other office-bearers—and the meetings are open for every member of the church to take part in the services, if they desire. But in Britain these weekly meetings are too much monopolized by the pastors. The result is that the ministers are overworked, the spiritual gifts of the church-members are not developed, and one great element of interest and profit disappears from the meetings. The social gatherings of a Christian Church ought to have the unrestrained freedom of a family. How preposterous it would seem if at a Christmas-dinner the "paterfamilias" should either monopolize the conversation or else allow each child to utter a syllable by special permission. Our American prayer-meetings are not faultless, but they are free from one very serious fault of the mid-week services of many of the English churches.

Two evenings previous to my sailing I visited Southport at the invitation of a dear friend who was once an active member of my Brooklyn church. Southport is an attractive suburb of Liverpool, with forty thousand residents, many of them doing business in the great city. During the evening I preached in the "West End Congregational Church" to an audience composed of various denominations. The edifice stood on a beautiful plat of verdure, surrounded by shrubbery and bright flower-beds. We have something to learn from our English kinsfolk in the matter of adorning the grounds around their sanctuaries; it is not only the ivy upon the walls, but the well-trimmed grass, and flowers beside the walls that make many a house of God so picturesque in its settings. While at Liverpool I was pained to learn that the Rev. Dr. Maclaren the brilliant Baptist preacher of Manchester is now laid aside, by ill health, from his pulpit. Among all the volumes of discourses that have come over to us lately in America none have excelled his in fresh suggestiveness of thought or felicity of style. They possess many of the rare merits of Frederick W. Robertson without any of Robertson's idiosyncracies in theology.

When conversing with my fellow-passengers I find that their Sabbath experiences have often resembled my own. Over much of the Continent the only opportunity for Americans to hear the gospel in their own tongue is afforded by the various chapels which have been opened by the churches of England or Scotland. Outside of Paris, these are commonly very dry services. At Dresden, for example, I went to a chapel where the minister conducted the service in a most lifeless way—his voice being about as audible as the faint squeak of a mouse in the wall. At the close the congregation sang "Jerusalem the golden" with heartiness, and that was really the only satisfaction which the otherwise inanimate service afforded me. It reminded me of the stranger who was bluntly asked by the minister, "Well, what did you think of my preaching this morning?" and the ingenuous reply was, "I thought you gave us two good psalms." If it were not for uniting with fellow-Christians in divine worship and listening to God's Word either read or sung, one might almost as well abide with his Bible in the quiet of his lodging-room. Why is it that these chapel-services are so often a perfunctory formality and that such meagre diet is afforded to travellers who become especially hungry for a good sermon while in a strange land?

Among the pleasant company on board of the Algeria is Professor Thorold Rogers of Oxford and the Member of Parliament for the borough of Southwark. He is a brilliant converser as well as an able political economist; during our civil war he warmly espoused the side of Union and Emancipation. Perhaps he enjoys the generous fare on board all the more from his having been kept on "Irish stew" for the last three months in Parliament. The English Church is represented by Canon Prichard, and by the Rev. James McCormick the portly and genial Vicar of Kingston-on-Hull. Mr. M. tells me that no two men in the Established Church rank higher for the best qualities of head and heart than the present Archbishops of Canterbury and York. Those two eminent sees have seldom been so ably filled, or with men more staunch in their devotion to sound doctrine. I was sorry that during my sojourn in London I failed to hear Dr. Magee the eloquent Bishop of Peterborough who is famous both for his impulsive oratory and his Irish humor. When I made the attempt at Westminster Abbey, the crowd were blockading the doorways an half hour before the time of service, and thousands, like myself, went away, unable to gain admission.

Many stories are current of the Bishop's Hibernian pleasantries. The Archbishop of Canterbury (Dr. Tait) once said to him, "Bishop Magee, I fancy that I am also of Irish lineage, and that my family may date back to the days of Brian Boroimhe." The Bishop of Peterborough waggishly replied— "Well, I never heard that we had any Taits in Ireland, but we have plenty of *taters*."

Of the preachers in the Established Church none are more widely known than Canon Farrar of Westminster, and Canon Liddon of St. Paul's. Dr. Farrar attracts great crowds on every Sabbath that he preaches in the Abbey—; Americans always contributing their full share to the throng. He is a tall, manly intellectual-looking personage in the pulpit and speaks with much earnestness. His unsatisfactory utterances on Future Retribution have excited some prejudice among the Low Church party, and he is considered as rather too radical by the Tory High Church party. But his superb volumes—the Life of Christ, and the Life of

St. Paul—and his fearless assaults upon the drinking-usages, of England have won for him the enthusiastic admiration of tens of thousands on both sides of the Atlantic. He is a large-hearted and lovable man, with a prodigious capacity for hard work. The rising man in London among the distinctively "Low Church" is Rev. W. Boyd Carpenter, who preaches in the neighborhood of Hyde Park. Dr. Edward Bickersteth, so well known by his "Yesterday, To-day and Forever" has a parish on Hampstead Hill. The Low Church are a minority in the Church of England, but on the bench of Bishops they are represented by several men of fervent piety, and eminent culture. The influence of such prelates as Thomson, Fraser, Tait, Lightfoot Ellicott and Ryle "tells" most effectively for evangelical truth. The Presbyterian pulpit in London is most ably manned by such men as Dr. Oswald Dykes (the successor of Dr. James Hamilton) Dr. Donald Fraser, Dr. Edmunds, and Dr. Sinclair Patterson. The Orthodox Quakers in

England are to be *weighed* rather than counted; although few in numbers they accomplish, in their quiet way, no small amount of solid good.

Some of my readers may wonder why the pastor of a Presbyterian flock has not turned his footsteps towards either Switzerland or Scotland. But I have paid several visits to those countries in former years; and during my present tour, I had determined to seek out only those localities with which (excepting London) I was not already familiar. The brief inspection I have made of several lands has confirmed some previous opinions, but has led me to revise others quite materially. Travel dispels some illusions, and discovers unexpected beauties; there were places in the East which I had thought of as verdant Arcadias which proved to be but barren rocks or inhospitable mountains. The best portions of Palestine are better than I expected to find them; its worst portions are desolate beyond all conception. Over the near future of that land, so tenderly dear to all Christian hearts, hangs an unlifted mystery. The prospects of both Egypt and Syria are brightening under the steady introduction of Occidental ideas. In the development of those Arabic-speaking nations, the American college and the mission-presses of Beyrout are to play an important part. Mohammedanism is not the inert and moribund system which we in America so generally regard it. On the contrary it holds its own in Asia and is aggressive in Africa. Only on European soil does it show signs of decay. As it sprung from the powerful brain of one man, so, in the Providence of God, one or more men may arise within its domain who may do unto Islam what Luther did unto Romanism in the heart of Europe.

The Greeks impressed me as being the rising race in the Levant. Greece as a war-like power is not formidable, but Greek merchants are growing rich by commerce and erelong will make Athens one of the most brilliant cities on the Mediterranean

Turkey when seen close at hand is no less detestable than when seen at a distance. The sooner that the "sick man" is carried across the Bosphorus, the sooner will Bulgaria advance to her rightful position and the sooner will disorderly Albania become a habitable country. All through the Orient —yes, and all through Europe the perpetual eye-sore is the ubiquitous *soldier.* In his various uniforms, white, scarlet, or blue, he is everywhere. Except in their modern equipments these colossal standing armies seem like monstrous relics of the dark ages. Certainly in our time the sword does not shape as if it were turning into a ploughshare. Whatever were my impressions of various countries, one thing is very clear, and that is that the American Republic is making a prodigious impression upon the older continents. It is not merely the coming nation; *it has come!* The great battle-field of the next century lies between Plymouth Rock and San Francisco. If the Devil gets America, the progress of humanity goes back more than ten degrees on the dial-plate. If the Lord Jesus Christ gets America, then all the sooner will the Millennial dawning break. It is not a matter for empty boasting, but it is a matter of momentous responsibility to be an American citizen and to bear even the humblest part in shaping its moral destiny.

Our delightful voyage draws to its close, and the atmosphere takes on a brighter hue. The leaden clouds have been left behind us; the fog-whistle has ceased to disturb our slumbers, and to-day we have the foretokens of home in a sapphire sky and a smiling sea. To-morrow morning the captain promises that we may pasture our eyes on the verdure of Staten Island. Then farewell to the Bible-lands that I have left far beyond these waves—and hail to the home and hearts around that church-spire which glitters in the morning sun! How sweetly natural was the prayer of that absent shepherd who was yearning to meet his folk—

"That I may come unto you with joy, by the will of God, and may, together with you, be refreshed."

INDEX.

Adolphus Gustavus........... 250
Ajalon........ 83
Alexandria.... 43
Alford.........................333
" his inn....'...... .. . 334
Arab Village... 48
" Footmen...................56
" Beggars...................91
" Court.....................66
" S. S......................6
Apollos 147
Archimedes 39
Arnold.........................20
Athens........................160
" Acropolis...........162, 175
" Parthenon..........162, 175
Bazaars........................62
Barclay...................98, 111
Batcheller................50, 66
Bescow........................242
Bethany..................94, 106
Bethlehem......................99
Beyroot.......................132
Bernandotte...................240
Bliss...................135, 154
Bothnia........................19
Brenner Pass..................188
Broady...................243, 254
Burns....................12, 319
Bunyan........................267
Butter, by Pint...............329
Brassy Praise 321
Byron...................178, 282
Caernarvon....................339
Cairo......................46, 55
Calvary.......................121
Capri..........................37
Carlyle..................14, 272
Carmel........................131
Cattegat......................231
Chios.........................140
Chittenden....................134
Chapel Services...............349
Christians....................234

Clock, ancient................315
Copenhagen....................220
Constantinople................150
Connaught, Duke...............278
Cook, Joseph..................312
Cook, Thomas..........45, 80, 88
Corsica........................30
Cowper...................20, 268
Crete..........................41
Cyprus.........................41
Cunarders................15, 83
Customs.......................152
Czar and Lincoln..............248
Dancing Dervishes..............59
Dead Sea......................102
De Lesseps.....................79
Devonshire....................313
Dijon..........................25
D'Grasli.......................23
Dodge, W. E..............134, 324
Drink Question................300
Dresden.......................195
Durer, A......................197
Ebal...........................83
Egypt, progress................63
E. Osinore....................231
Ephesus.......................143
Euroclydon.....................40
Farrar.............280, 292, 351
Fisk..........................137
Floraldial....................274
Garibaldi......................36
Garfield......................269
Gateman, polite................24
Gehenna.......................110
Gethsemane................92, 106
Gladstone.......... 23, 277, 296
Goshen.........................78
Gotha Canal...................255
Gothenburg......... 233, 260, 307
Greeks........................355
Hall, Newman........21, 275, 278
Hamlin........................156
Hamburg.......................212

Heat	50, 72
Hill, R	2
Innsbruck	189, 303
Jerusalem	87, 117
Jesuits	29, 35, 40
Jews	114
Jordan	105
Jericho	105
Jessup	132
Joppa	80, 129
Johnson, S	283
July F urth	147
Kenn, T	317
Kinnard	335
Kinney, W. B.	248
Lansing	70
Lawson, W	268
Lindblom	254
Lincoln's Murder	248
Llanberris	339
Luther	199, 201
Maclaren	348
Magoon	332
Marvel, A	273
Mason, Lowell	255
Marseilles	25, 27
Mc Mickan	10, 20
McAll	31
Melancthon	203
Milton	274, 321
Missions, 64, 68, 71, 80, 113, 127, 168	
Moody, D. L	133
Moriah	89
Morley	335
Moses	65
Naples	33
Napoleon	30, 43, 79, 182, 199, 236.
Nell Gwynn	272
Nelson	43
Noble, W	331
Norway	227
Olivet	84
Oscar II	241
Oil, Pratt's	128
Palestine Changing	109, 124
Palmquist	244, 254
Palmerston	328
Paris	25
Paul	39, 139, 146, 173, 179
Peck	217
Peel, R	21
Pencil and Plow	265
Peter	75
Pentelicus	169
Post	134
Prague	192
Prayerbook	14
Prohibition	79
Protesta m	26
Puteoli	39
Pyramids	51, 73
Queen Victoria	275
Raphael	196
Railroad Scenes	47
Rembrandt	196
Revision N. T.	329
Richardson, B. W.	311
Robert College	155
Robinson, E.	298
Rogers, T.	349
Seasick	43
Sedan	26
Sermon Making	290
Schaff	76
Scutari	153
Scylla and Charybdis	38
Schleiman	149, 164
Shaftesbury	326
Siloam	90
Sites, Ancient	120
Southport	347
Smith Eli	137
Smith, S. F.	244, 248, 255
Smyrna	142
Spurgeon	276, 288, 331
Stanley	292
Stewards, French	28
Stromboli	38
Stockholm	239
St. Sophia	153
Stevens	247
Sultan, a Nuisance	158, 355
Sunday, Stormy	12
Swedenborg	249
Talking by Interpreter	246
Talmud	116
Te Deum	316
Thwing, E. P.	235, 244
Thorwaldsden	189, 220
Trieste	183
Trolhattan	259
Vandyke	133, 198
Venice	184
Vesuvius	33, 37
Watts	286
Wells	315
Wenner Lake	259
Wesley	280
Wittenburg	201, 207
Wood	154
Y. M. C. A	235, 287, 323
Zion	84, 88

www.ingramcontent.com/pod-product-compliance
Lightning Source LLC
Chambersburg PA
CBHW020316240426
43673CB00039B/826